THOMAS TRENKLER

THE VIENNA HOFBURG

THE HISTORY
THE BUILDINGS
THE SIGHTS

UEBERREUTER

Showpiece of the Treasury: The Imperial Crown (1602)

Contents

HISTORY

TOUR

INSTITUTIONS

ENVIRONS

The Residence of the Habsburgs

The Hofburg was originally built as a fortress by Otakar II
Přemysl, the king of Bohemia, who had begun construction
by 1275. But it is inseparable from the House of Habsburg,
a family of Alemannic counts who came from the Habichts-
burg ("Hawk's Castle") in Aargau, in what is now Switzer-
land. Rudolf I, who had been elected German king in 1273,
is said to have moved into the Hofburg in 1279. In 1918,
after Austria had been defeated in World War I, the reign of
the Habsburg Dynasty over Austria, which with Hungary
had formed the Dual Monarchy, came to an end.
Over this period of just under 640 years, the Hofburg
developed into a magnificent, if heterogeneous, residence,
the center of a multinational empire and a monument to
Austrian and Western history. In the Hofburg the Congress
of Vienna was held, reorganizing Europe; here the precious
symbols of the Holy Roman Empire of the German Nation
were kept. This is where Maria Theresa and Sisi lived, Ludwig van Beethoven and Johann Strauss conducted, Antonio
Salieri and Anton Bruckner composed. Since 1498, the
Hofburg has been the home of the Vienna Boys' Choir and
since 1562, that of the Lipizzaner horses as well.
Almost every ruler continued to expand the Hofburg. During the Renaissance period, at the end of the 16th century,
it consisted of three separate buildings: the fortress (today

From the roof of the Neue Burg: St. Michael's Church and St. Stephen's Cathedral

the Schweizerhof ➤ Swiss Court); the residence of Maximilian II, which he adapted to stable his horses (the Stallburg); and the Amalienburg (named for the widow of Joseph I, Amalia of Brunswick). During the Baroque period, it grew into an ensemble of magnificent buildings (including the Court Library). The term "Hofburg" (literally: "court castle") was first used at the end of the 17th century. Each emperor in turn added new wings or remodeled existing apartments, because it was not customary to use the same rooms as one's immediate predecessor.

Thus every era left its traces behind – and every political system as well. The Hofburg, which today extends from the Albertina to Michaelertor (Michael's Gate) and on to the Offices of the Austrian President and from the Stallburg to Heldenplatz (Heroes' Square), the Kunsthistorisches and Naturhistorisches Museums (Museums of Art History and Natural History, respectively) and on to the Imperial Court Stables (now the MuseumsQuartier), has still not stopped growing, either above or below ground. Giant underground storage areas have been built and most recently, at the turn of the millennium, the MuseumsQuartier along with the new buildings of the Leopold Museum, the Kunsthalle Wien and the Museum of Modern Art.

With its 18 wings, 54 stairways, 19 courtyards and 2600 rooms, the Hofburg is the world's largest secular residential district. Together with the MuseumsQuartier it occupies an area of more than 500,000 m² (5,400,000 square feet), making it the world's largest complex of museums and monuments (with the possible exception of the Roman Forum). The museums and the Austrian National Library, which were founded for the most part on the collections of the Habsburgs, contain not only artworks from classical antiquity to the present but also magnificent weapons, precious manuscripts and extraordinary finds (papyrus documents, minerals and ethnological materials).

Practical Information

ADMISSION TICKETS: There is no general admission ticket for all the facilities in the Hofburg and MuseumsQuartier. There are individual tickets and several types of combination tickets (i.e. for the Kunsthistorisches Museum, the Schatzkammer (Treasury), the collections in the Neue Burg and the Austrian Theatre Museum, or for the Leopold Museum, the Museum of Modern Art, the Architekturzentrum and the Kunsthalle Wien). The ticket for the Imperial Apartments and the Sisi Museum is also valid for visiting the Imperial Silver Collection.

GUIDED TOURS: The organization "Walks in Vienna" offers several guided tours to the Hofburg with a focus on various aspects. Survey tour: every Sunday at 11:15 a.m., from April to October also every Wednesday at 10:30 a.m. (meeting place: Michaelerplatz near the excavations). Internet: www.wienguide.at, e-mail: office@wienfuehrung.at

CASH DISPENSERS: Raiffeisen, Michaelerplatz (corner of Kohlmarkt). MuseumsQuartier Main Entrance, Museumsplatz 1. Bank Austria Creditanstalt, Babenbergerstrasse 9.

KINDERINFO (CHILDREN'S INFORMATION): WienXtra-Kinderinfo is located in the MuseumsQuartier (in the wing between the Main Courtyard and Fürstenhof). It provides free information about leisure activities for children ages three to 13. Opening times: Tuesday to Thursday 2 p.m. to 7 p.m., Friday to Sunday 10 a.m. to 5 p.m. Phone: +43/1/4000-84 400. Internet: www.kinderinfowien.at.

MUSEUMSQUARTIER: phone: +43/1/523 58 81-1730, Infoline: 0820/600 600 (only in Austria), Internet: www.mqw.at. At the Main Entrance MQ Point (Info Tickets Shop), baby changing room, lost & found and free wheelchair service. Tours of the grounds: German, English, French, Italian and Spanish by prior arrangement at tour@mqw.at.

PUBLIC TRANSPORTATION: The quickest way to reach the Hofburg is by subway (U-Bahn) line U3 (station: Herrengasse). The MuseumsQuartier is next to the Volkstheater station of the U2 and U3. Bus line 2A connects the Hofburg with the Kunsthistorisches and Naturhistorisches Museums and the MQ (only until 8 p.m., on Saturday until 7 p.m.; bus does not operate on Sunday).

PARKING: Underground parking is provided right in front of the MuseumsQuartier (Museumsplatz). A reduction is available upon purchase of an MQ combination ticket. More underground parking is located at the Staatsoper, Rathausplatz (Dr. Karl-Lueger-Ring) and on Stiftgasse behind the MuseumsQuartier. Parking on Heldenplatz is usually only permitted with special permission (Wagenkarte).

POLICE: Goethegasse 1, phone: +43/1/313 10-21330. Stiftgasse 2a, phone: +43/1/313 10-22380.

POST OFFICES: A-1014 Vienna, Wallnerstrasse 5–7. A-1016 Vienna, Museumsstrasse 12.

TAXIS: On Reitschulgasse (next to Michaelerplatz), on Bellariastrasse and at the lower end of Mariahilfer Strasse.

Shops

CHEAP RECORDS & STORE in the Fischer von Erlach Wing on Electric Avenue (MQ). Opening times: Tuesday to Friday 12:30 p.m. to 7 p.m., Saturday and Sunday 1 p.m. to 6 p.m. Records and CDs, designer merchandise.

Next to the MQ's Main Entrance: Prachner Bookshop

KULTURBUCHHANDLUNG PRACHNER (cultural bookshop) in the Fischer von Erlach Wing next to the MQ-Point. Opening times: Monday to Saturday 10 a.m. to 7 p.m., Sundays and holidays 1 p.m. to 7 p.m. Books and magazines (architecture, art, landscape architecture, photography, Austrian themes).

LOMOSHOP next to the Kunsthalle Wien Shop (MQ) underneath the open-air staircase to the Museum of Modern Art. Opening times: daily 1 p.m. to 7 p.m. Various cameras, novelty items, gifts.

MÄDCHENPOP and LA FÁBRICA DE LA SUERTE in the Fischer von Erlach Wing on Electric Avenue (MQ). Opening times: Tuesday to Friday 1 p.m. to 7 p.m., Saturday and Sunday noon to 6 p.m. Fashion and the other things girls need.

MQ POINT (INFO & TICKET SHOP) in the Fischer von Erlach Wing at the Main Entrance (MQ). Opening times: daily 10 a.m. to 7 p.m. Information and brochures about the MQ, admission tickets, MQ products, gifts, toys, jewelry.

MUSEUM SHOPS in the Albertina, Architekturzentrum Wien (MQ), Imperial Apartments, Kunsthalle Wien (MQ), Kunsthistorisches Museum, Leopold Museum (MQ), Lipizzaner Museum, Museum of Modern Art (MQ), Naturhistorisches Museum, Treasury and Spanish Riding School. Opening times are usually the same as those of the respective institution.

SOUVENIR SHOPS in the pedestrian arcade between Heldenplatz and the inner courtyard (In der Burg). Opening times: generally Monday to Friday 9 a.m. to 6 p.m.; closing times on weekends are generally earlier.

TABAK TRAFIK (TOBACCONIST'S SHOPS) in the pedestrian arcade between Heldenplatz and the inner courtyard (In der Burg). Opening times: daily 8 a.m. to 6 p.m. Tobacco products, newspapers, magazines, souvenirs, postcards.

Cafés and Restaurants

AUGUSTINERKELLER and WEINMUSEUM next to the Albertina. Opening times: Sunday to Friday 11 a.m. to midnight, Saturday 11 a.m. to 3 p.m. Phone: +43/1/533 10 26. Traditional restaurant (Viennese cuisine) with new wine on tap.

CAFÉ ATELIER next to the escalator to the Albertina. Opening times: daily 8 a.m. to 2 a.m. Phone: +43/1/533 10 26. Café and bar. Outdoor seating.

CAFÉ LEOPOLD in the Leopold Museum (MQ). Opening times: daily 10 a.m. to 2 a.m. (Thursday to Saturday 10 a.m. to 4 a.m.). Phone: +43/1/523 67 32. Café, bar and restaurant with moderate prices (snacks, midday set meal). Two outdoor seating areas. DJ lines on weekends.

CAFÉ NAUTILUS in the Cupola Hall of the Naturhistorisches Museum (Maria-Theresien-Platz). Opening times: daily except Tuesday 10 a.m. to 6 p.m. Phone: +43/1/524 02 50. Café and restaurant.

CAFÉ RESTAURANT HALLE is located in the Kaiserloge (Emperor's Box) in the former Winter Riding Hall (MQ). Opening times: daily 10 a.m. to 2 a.m. (hot dishes until 11:30 p.m., Friday and Saturday until midnight). Phone: +43/1/523 70 01. Mediterranean cuisine, breakfast until 4 p.m. Two outdoor seating areas.

CAFÉ SPANISCHE HOFREITSCHULE on Michaelerplatz. Opening times: as a rule Tuesday to Sunday 9 a.m. to 5 p.m. Phone: +43/1/533 41 11. Operated by the Sacher Hotel. View of the Summer Riding School through the window.

DO & CO in the Albertina. Opening times: daily 10 a.m. to midnight. Phone: +43/1/532 96 69. Café, bar and restaurant (expensive). Outdoor seating on the Bastion.

EL MUSEO in the Museum of Modern Art (MQ). Opening times: daily 10 a.m. to 2 a.m. (hot dishes until 11:30 p.m.), Thursday to Saturday 10 a.m. to 4 a.m. Phone: +43/1/525 00 1440. Café and restaurant, Mediterranean and Latin American cuisine, clubbing, outdoor seating.

GERSTNER in the Cupola Hall of the Kunsthistorisches Museum (Maria-Theresien-Platz). Opening times: daily except Monday

In the Cupola Hall of the Naturhistorisches Museum: Café Nautilus

In the Burggarten: Palmenhaus Brasserie and Bar

10 a.m. to 6 p.m. (evening buffet on Thursday until 11 p.m.). Phone: +43/1/526 13 61. Café and restaurant.

GLACIS-BEISL at the Breite Gasse entrance (MQ). Opening times: daily 11 a.m. to 2 a.m. Traditional restaurant (Viennese cuisine), recently refurbished. Outdoor seating (unfortunately no longer as enchanting as it was before the MQ was built).

HOFBURG CAFÉ near the Imperial Apartments (In der Burg). Opening times: daily 9 a.m. to 8 p.m. Fine café-restaurant with outdoor seating.

HOFBURGSTÜBERL in the pedestrian arcade between Heldenplatz and the Inner Courtyard (In der Burg). Opening times: Monday to Friday 7 a.m. to 5 p.m., Saturday, Sunday and holidays 10 a.m. to 3 p.m. Stand-up snack bar.

KANTINE (cafeteria) in the Fischer von Erlach Wing (MQ). Opening times: Sunday to Wednesday 10 a.m. to midnight, Thursday to Saturday 10 a.m. to 2 a.m. Phone: +43/1/523 82 39. Snacks, including filled pita pockets, inexpensive daily plate (also vegetarian). Two outdoor seating areas.

MEIEREI in the Volksgarten. Opening times: April 1 to October 30, roughly 9 a.m. to 8 p.m. (depending on the weather). Phone: +43/1/533 21 05. Café, pastries and snacks. Formerly housed a water reservoir. Outdoor seating.

MQ-Daily (Under'm Hollerbusch) in the Fischer von Erlach Wing (MQ). Opening times: Monday to Friday 9 a.m. to 7 p.m., Saturday 9 a.m. to 6 p.m. Phone: +43/1/526 53 03. Food, beverages, take-out dishes and fixed midday meal of organic products.

Palmenhaus in the Burggarten. Opening times: daily 10 a.m. to 2 a.m. (closed Mondays and Tuesdays from November to February). Phone: +43/1/533 10 33. Café, brasserie and bar in a Jugendstil greenhouse. Large outdoor seating area.

Restaurant Una near the Architekturzentrum Wien (MQ). Opening times: Monday to Saturday 9 a.m. to midnight (hot dishes 9:30 a.m. to 10:30 p.m.), Saturday, Sunday and holidays 10 a.m. to 6 p.m. Phone: +43/1/523 65 66. Chic, with ceiling faced with Turkish tiles. Outdoor seating.

Soho in the Neue Burg (entrance: Bibliothekshof). Opening times: Monday to Friday 9 a.m. to 4 p.m. (closed August). Phone: +43/676/309 51 61. Reasonably priced cafeteria of the Austrian National Library. Fine set meals at midday.

Volksgarten Clubdiskothek on Burgring. Opening times: as a rule starting at 11 p.m. Phone: +43/1/532 42 41. Bar and disco. Well preserved furnishings from the 1950s. Outdoor seating (café with dancing on summer weekends).

Volksgarten Pavilion. Opening times: April to September daily 10 a.m. to 2 a.m. Phone: +43/1/532 09 07. Espresso bar from the 1950s, in its original condition. Outdoor seating.

Faced with Turkish tiles: Una in the MuseumsQuartier

The History of the Hofburg

Prologue: The End of the Babenbergs

The Babenberg ruler Henry II Jasomirgott, who in 1156 had obtained for Austria the status of a duchy from Emperor Frederick I Barbarossa, built a palace in his new capital, Vienna. The building and walls surrounded a courtyard, today the square Am Hof. Under his son Leopold V and succeeding rulers, the ducal palace, which has vanished today, was expanded. It was financed in part with the English ransom paid for the release of Richard the Lion-Hearted, who was captured in Vienna in 1193 while returning from the Holy Land.

With the death of Frederick II on June 15, 1246, in the battle against the Hungarians at the Leitha River, the male line of the Babenberg family, which had ruled since 976, came to an end. In 1252, Frederick's sister Margaret, a widow since 1242, married Otakar II Přemysl of Bohemia, who assumed power in Vienna and expanded his sphere of influence from the Sudeten region to the Adriatic. But when he was excluded from voting in the 1273 election that chose Rudolf of Habsburg (1218–1291) to be the first German king (king of the Romans), he refused to recognize Rudolf. In 1276 the Imperial Diet launched a military campaign against Otakar, and Rudolf I marched on Vienna with an army of 20,000. The decisive Battle of Dürnkrut took place in 1278 on the Marchfeld plain, and Otakar was killed as he tried to flee.

The Fortress of Otakar II

By 1275 the king of Bohemia had begun construction of a fortress within the Vienna city wall (built between 1200 and 1207) on an elevation next to the Widmer Gate. It was a complex with four towers around a rectangular courtyard, which today is called the Schweizerhof (Swiss Court). Rudolf I is said to have moved into the fortress in 1279 because the ducal fortress of the Babenbergs had become uninhabitable following a large fire in 1276. His son Albert (1248–1308) built the Castle Chapel (first mentioned in 1296). To the southeast of the fortress, the Church of the Augustinian Friars was consecrated in 1349. There were two reasons why no other major architectural changes occurred during this period: firstly, the construction of St. Stephen's Cathedral required large sums of money, and secondly, Vienna had lost importance with the division of the Habsburg lands (1379). The fortress was then used only occasionally as a residence. The only major change occurred when Albert V (1379–1439) rebuilt the chapel (1423–1426). In 1452, Frederick III (1415–1493), who preferred Wiener Neustadt as his residence, was crowned emperor of the Holy Roman Empire by the Pope. The title remained in the Habsburg family (with a brief interruption between 1742 and 1745) until the Empire came to an end in 1806. In 1488, the "House of Austria" was reunited for 76 years. Maximilian I (1459–1519), the "Last Knight," was the founder of the Habsburg practice of conducting politics through matrimony. His motto was: *"Bella gerant alii, tu felix Austria nube"* ("Let others wage wars: you, fortunate Austria, marry"). In 1477, Maximilian married Mary of Burgundy, heiress to the rich duchy to which the Netherlands also belonged. His son Philip (1478–1506) married Joan, the heiress of Castile and Aragon, bringing Spain with its colonies in South America into the Habsburg realm. Ferdinand I (1503–1564), a grandson of Maximilian, married Anna, heiress to the kingdoms of Bohemia and Hungary. Thus within three generations the Habsburgs were in possession of a world empire on which "the sun never set." Ferdinand I made Vienna the capital of the archduchy. Following the Turkish siege of 1529, he built a ring of bastions and curtains along the ring wall in 1531. The bastion called

Mid-16th century: the Schweizertor (Swiss Gate) by Pietro Ferrabosco and on the right, the wing for the children of Ferdinand I

the Burg Bastion and later the "Spanier" (Spanish Bastion) was built in front of the Widmer Gate. Significant changes were also made within the fortress: the three existing wings were extended outwards and upwards, and the fortified wall on the northwest was replaced by a fourth wing with the Schweizertor (Swiss Gate, built in 1552, probably by Pietro Ferrabosco). Because there was still a shortage of space, a wing was added on the southwest, above the Widmer Gate and beyond, for Ferdinand's children (the "Kinderstöckl"). On the side towards the city, the Burgplatz (Castle Square), on which tournaments were held, was bordered by several buildings that housed the newly constituted administration, including the Court Treasury and the Court Chancellery. On the northwest, the Cillierhof, which had burned almost to the ground in 1525, was repaired and restored to its use as an armoury. Other additions were a room of natural arts and wonders in the palace, a hospital north of the Cillierhof, a corridor from the palace to the Church of the Augustinian Friars and a new Real (Royal) Tennis Court, because the old one had been destroyed in a devastating fire. This was a type of tennis that Ferdinand I had learned to play in Spain.

The Stallburg and the Amalienburg

In 1559, Ferdinand began building a residence for his son on the grounds of an abandoned church east of the palace. Construction of the free-standing building, however, proceeded slowly. Following the death of his father in 1564, Maximilian II (1527–1576) moved into the old residence, converting the new building to provide a stable for his Spanish horses. To this building, known as the Stallburg, a second storey was added in 1565. Hardly any changes were made to the fortress itself, which according to contemporary accounts must have been quite ugly. In 1554, Ferdinand I decided to divide the Habsburg lands among his three sons, which once again diminished the importance of Vienna. Maximilian II, who in addition to "Austria above and below the Enns River" had also received Bohemia and Hungary, spent much of his time in Prague. A year before his death in 1576, he decided to erect a new building to provide a court for his eldest son, replacing the Cillierhof. The armoury moved to Renngasse. But instead of holding court in Vienna, the son, Rudolf II (1552–1612), moved his residence to Prague. As governor, his brother Ernest occupied the third large free-standing building, which was constructed between 1575 and 1577. (The name the building has today, Amalienburg, was not used until the 18th century: the widow of Joseph I, Amalia of Brunswick, moved there in 1711 after her husband's death.)

To house the treasury and art collections, Rudolf II built a new wing (1583–1585) on the northeast of the palace. It was a three-storey building located behind the Real Tennis Court. Expansion of the Amalienburg continued until 1610–1611. Following the death of Rudolf II, his brother Matthias (1557–1619) moved his residence back to Vienna, but because of the Thirty Years' War few changes were made to the Hofburg. Under Ferdinand II (1578–1637) a ballroom was built (1629–1631) where the two Redoutensäle now stand. Most likely this was done at the request of Empress Eleonora Gonzaga.

This building, probably a wooden structure, was converted by Giovanni Burnacini between 1659 and 1660 into a theatre with the latest stage technology. He was commissioned to do so by Leopold I (1640–1705), who ruled for almost half a century (starting in 1657). On the occasion of Leopold's marriage to the infanta Margaret Theresa of Spain in 1666, a new three-tiered opera house with seating for 5000 was built on the "Cortina" (curtain) of the city wall in the area of what is today the Burggarten. The wedding is said to have been one of the most lavish celebrations ever staged in the Hofburg.

Mid-17th century: the Amalienburg with the Minorite Church behind it

The Leopoldine Wing

Leopold I was interested in far more than just Italian
Baroque opera and theatre: in 1660 he decided to remodel

The Burghauptmannschaft

By virtue of its dimensions, the Hofburg with its 18 wings,
54 stairways and 19 courtyards is like a small town. It is
administered by the Burghauptmannschaft, a department
of the Economic Ministry. Among its duties are the nego-
tiation and signing of rental agreements (there are around
50 apartments and several shops in the Hofburg), planning
and supervising all construction activities, and maintaining
the building complex. It also operates its own fire service,
which is responsible for safety.

The first mention of a *Burggraf* (burgrave) appointed to
command the Hofburg (Michael von Maidburg) dates
from the year 1434. The name *"Burghauptmann"* to des-
ignate the office was used for the first time in 1443. In
1793, Francis II/I declined to nominate a burgrave, and
those duties were then performed by a *"Burginspektor"*
or castle inspector. In 1849, Emperor Francis Joseph I
authorized a basic reform of court services. Subsequently
the *"Hofburginspektion"* was renamed *"Burghauptmannschaft."* In 1850 Ludwig Montoyer was appointed
director of the newly created department. He was the
son of the court architect, Louis Montoyer. According to
a detailed description of duties, which remained valid
until the downfall of the monarchy in 1918, the
Burghauptmannschaft had responsibility for taking care of
the building complex itself but also for its furniture, security and cleaning. In 1870, Montoyer was succeeded by
Ferdinand Kirschner, who deserves credit for the completion of the Michaelertrakt (Michael's Wing).

Since 2001, the Burghauptmannschaft has been responsible
not only for the Hofburg, including the Albertina, Kunsthistorisches and Naturhistorisches Museums, but also for
all state-owned historical buildings in Austria. These
include the palaces in Marchfeld, the former Nazi concentration camp at Mauthausen, the Federal Chancellery,
Belvedere Palace and several other palaces in Vienna, the
Heldenberg (an Austrian Army memorial), the Hofburg in
Innsbruck and Ambras Castle in Tirol. Around 180
employees administer all of these buildings and facilities.

the Hofburg and the courtyard that is now called "In der Burg." Modeled on the new residence in Munich, a long winged building was completed in 1667 between the Kindertrakt (Children's Wing) and the Amalienburg. Based on plans by Philiberto Lucchese, it replaced a section of the city wall. In February 1668, a large fire broke out that almost completely destroyed the new wing. The Jews were accused of arson, and in 1670 at the request of his wife, Margaret Theresa, Leopold I ordered the ghetto to be evacuated and closed in the "Corpus Christi expulsion." Since that time, the district has been called the "Leopoldstadt." By 1681, the Leopoldine Wing was rebuilt by Giovanni Pietro Tencala: it was a third longer than before and a mezzanine storey was added. In addition, the Widmer Tower was incorporated into the façade, so that the building was no longer free-standing. The design of the façade, which was identical to that of the previous building and harmonized with the old palace, was intended to create architectural uniformity.

The riding-school building on the Exercise Ground to the southeast of the palace was not renovated until the Leopoldine Wing had been completed, although plans had existed since 1663. A library floor was added, making it essentially the predecessor of the Court Library. The constant threat of attack from the east had ended with the defeat of the Turks in 1683. For the first time, it was possible to consider converting the Hofburg, which was still a fortress, into a more ostentatious building complex. Leopold I commissioned Johann Lucas von Hildebrandt, who had been Imperial Court Engineer since 1700, to create a model for the new complex. This project, however, was never realized. The Emperor had meanwhile become more interested in a new hunting lodge, which was built between 1695 and 1711 according to plans by Johann Bernhard Fischer von Erlach. The only changes made by Leopold's elder son, Joseph I (1678–1711), were to demolish the south tower, to replace the old sacristy of the Castle Chapel with a new addition, and to connect the Leopoldine Wing to the Amalienburg, which meanwhile had risen to a height of four storeys. Although Fischer von Erlach tutored the Emperor in architecture and was Inspektor der Kaiserlichen Gebäude (Supervisor of Imperial Buildings), architecture remained rather neglected as an art form at Joseph's court. That changed suddenly after his premature death. His brother Charles VI (1685–1740), who had been king of Spain since 1703,

Johann Bernhard Fischer von Erlach

was baptized on July 20, 1656, in St.
Martin near Graz and died on April
5, 1723, in Vienna. After training as a
sculptor with his father, he turned to
architecture. In 1670 he went to
Rome, where the work of Francesco
Borromini and Gian Lorenzo Bernini
deeply impressed him. In 1684 he
moved to Naples, returning to Graz
in 1686. Two years later he designed
Frain Palace in southern Moravia. From 1689 he taught architecture to the Prince Imperial, Joseph I, in Vienna. His first
design for Schönbrunn adopted the French style. From 1693,
he was employed by the Prince-Archbishop of Salzburg,
where his buildings include the Seminary with the Trinity
Church (Dreifaltigkeitskirche; 1694–1702) and the University
Church (Kollegienkirche; 1696–1707). In 1694 he was
appointed Imperial Court Architect and Engineer in Vienna. In
1795 construction began on his second design for Schönbrunn
Palace, completed in 1711. Raised to noble rank in 1696, the
first artist to be thus honored, he added the name of his
mother's first husband (Sebastian Erlacher) to his, calling himself "Fischer von Erlach." In the years that followed, he developed an increasingly independent style of intersecting building
wings, whose spatial concept frequently emanated from an
oval shape. In contrast to Johann Lukas von Hildebrandt, who
was a generation younger, he placed little importance on
sumptuous decoration. In 1705, following the accession of
Joseph I to the throne, Fischer von Erlach was appointed
Inspektor der Kaiserlichen Gebäude (Supervisor of Imperial
Buildings). Thus he was in charge of the entire imperial building enterprise. In 1712 he was confirmed in office by Charles
VI. In 1721 he published the first seminal monograph on architectural history. Entitled *Entwurf einer historischen Architektur* (*A
Plan of Civil and Historical Architecture*), it contained the reconstructed designs of famous buildings. His most important
buildings, besides the churches in Salzburg, are Clam-Gallas
Palace in Prague (1707–1712), Batthyány-Schönborn Palace
(1699–1711), the Böhmische Hofkanzlei (Bohemian Chancellery; 1708–1714) and Schwarzenberg Palace, which Hildebrandt had begun (completion 1720–1723) in Vienna. The
strict unity of Trautson Palace (1710–1716) pointed the way

to his culminating works in Vienna, the Karlskirche (Church of St. Charles Borromeo, begun in 1716) and the Hofbibliothek (Imperial Court Library, begun in 1722). Just as with the Imperial Stables, his son completed the latter two projects.

Joseph Emanuel Fischer von Erlach

was born on September 12, 1693, in Vienna, where he died on June 29, 1742. Following studies in Germany, Italy and probably in England and France as well, he returned to Vienna in 1722. A short time later he entered the service of Prince Schwarzenberg and took over supervision of the latter's palace from his father, who was gravely ill. In 1725 Charles VI appointed him to his father's office of Supervisor of Imperial Buildings, despite the opposition of Johann Lukas von Hildebrandt. His designs, such as the Reichskanzleitrakt (Imperial Chancellery Wing; 1726–30, which Hildebrandt had begun, and the Hofreitschule (Court Riding School, 1729–1735) in the Hofburg, were influenced by early French Classicism. He later abandoned architecture to pursue his technological talents as inventor, mine engineer and machine-builder.

Johann Lucas von Hildebrandt

was born on November 14, 1668, in Genoa and died on November 16, 1745, in Vienna. He studied with Carlo Fontana in Rome and was a fortifications engineer during the Italian campaigns of Prince Eugene of Savoy. Hildebrandt came to Vienna in 1696. In 1700 he became Court Engineer, in 1711 Director of the Court Department of Planning and Building, and in 1723 Court Architect. He was unable, however, to assert himself against the competition of the Fischers and worked primarily for the aristocracy: Among his buildings were Daun-Kinsky Palace (1713–1726) and Starhemberg-Schönburg Palace (1705–1706) as well as several palaces for

Prince Eugene, including the Lower (1714–1716) and grandiose Upper (1721–1723) Belvedere Palaces as well as completion of Prince Eugene's Winter Palace on Himmelpfortgasse (1702–1724), the core of which had been built by Johann Bernhard Fischer von Erlach (1695–1698). Other Vienna buildings designed by Hildebrandt are St. Peter's Church (1702), the Piarist Church of Maria Treu (1716) and the Geheime Hofkanzlei (Secret Chancellery, 1717–1719), today the Federal Chancellery. Compared to those of Johann Bernhard Fischer, Hildebrandt's buildings seem more pleasant and agreeable. The façades are often decorated with artistically entwined bands, uniting them in an artistic whole. Hildebrandt's architecture was widely popular in his day and had enormous lasting influence.

returned to Vienna in 1712 and immediately asked Hildebrandt to convert the gated structure between Kohlmarkt and the main courtyard into a monumental triumphal arch as a representative sign of imperial power. In 1714, Charles VI was forced to relinquish his claim to Spain (the Bourbons having won the War of the Spanish Succession). He maintained close ties to that country, however, and introduced Spanish court protocol in Vienna. Under his rule, the monarchy reached its greatest geographic expansion.

The Baroque Alterations

In 1713, Charles VI commissioned Fischer von Erlach, whom he had confirmed in office, to design the new Imperial Stables at the edge of the glacis, the defensive slope outside the city wall. Construction began in 1719. The model for the complex was Fischer von Erlach's reconstruction of Nero's Domus Aurea, the Golden House in Rome. The second project was construction of the new Court Library in 1722, built according to Fischer von Erlach's plans instead of a combined riding-school and library building.
With the death of Fischer in 1723, his most bitter rival, Johann Lucas von Hildebrandt, saw an opportunity to become involved in the remodeling of the Hofburg. In 1724 he presented the Emperor with a general plan that proposed striking alterations to the old fortress, including a large chapel in the courtyard. Hildebrandt's concept included a monumental façade facing the city, with sweeping corners, a rotunda and a cupola. But in 1725, Charles VI conferred the

office of Supervisor of Imperial Buildings upon Joseph Emanuel Fischer, who had already assumed responsibility from his father for the Imperial Stables and the Court Library. In the same year the palatial façade of the Imperial Stables was completed (the additional wings were never realized, the imperial stud having become too small to require them). The shell of the Court Library was finished by 1726, and in 1730 Daniel Gran completed his frescoes. It took until 1737 to completely furnish the building.

In 1723, the only contract remaining for Hildebrandt was building the new Imperial Chancellery, the planning of which he had begun the year before on a commission from the Imperial Chancellor. But even this wing was never completed according to his plans: in 1726 Charles VI took responsibility for the construction away from the Imperial Chancellor and entrusted it to his Court Chancellery in order to allow Joseph Emanuel Fischer to design the façade facing the Burgplatz, although, like the one facing Schauflergasse, it had already been erected. It was intended that Fischer should design the Court Treasury and thus the façade facing the Michaelerkirche (St. Michael's Church). The goal was twofold: a unification of the façades and a demonstration of power: the Imperial Chancellery Wing thus became a project of the Emperor and not of the Empire. Starting in 1728, following a two-year break in the planning, the Court Treasury and the façades of the two buildings were realized. But Michael's Wing with its dominant rotunda, for which Hildebrandt's triumphal arch had to step aside so to speak, remained incomplete. By the time construction was halted in 1735, only the southeastern section of the façade had been completed, with the Winterreitschule (Winter Riding Hall) stretched out behind it, having been built by Fischer between 1729 and 1733. The rotunda, which remained half-finished for the next one and a half centuries, resembled an ancient ruin.

In 1740 Maria Theresa (1717–1780), the eldest daughter of Charles VI, ascended the throne. In the first years of her reign she succeeded in defending her inheritance against France and Prussia, but she was forced to relinquish the wealthy region of Silesia. The Empress adopted the ideas of the Enlightenment, introduced compulsory school attendance for all children and abolished torture. She also continued the traditional Habsburg matrimonial policy, marrying off most of her children to royal families throughout Europe. In 1741, a year after her coronation, she converted the Ballhaus (Real Tennis Court), which stood between the Winter Riding Hall and the torso of the Round Tower, into the Court Theatre. In the 1770s the Theatre Wing facing Kohlmarkt was given a blind façade, furthering strengthening the picturesque appearance of St. Michael's Square. The new Ballhaus was built next to the Imperial Hospital and remained there until 1903, giving Ballhausplatz its name. The name Bellaria survived as well: the Empress, who lived and reigned (often from her bed) on the second floor ("bel étage") of the Leopoldine Wing, had a special ramp built so that she would not have to climb any stairs, calling it the Bellaria.

The Redoutensäle and Joseph's Square

Once the Court Theatre and the Winterreitschule (Winter Riding Hall) had been built, there was no longer any need for Burnacini's theatre. Between 1744 and 1748 it was converted according to plans by Jean-Nicolas Jadot into a large and a small ballroom, the Redoutensäle. A decade later, Maria Theresa's preferred architect, Nikolaus Pacassi, received a commission to renovate them for the

The Hofburg at the time of Maria Theresa (by Josef Daniel Huber 1776, detail): Court Library, Winter Riding Hall, Court Theatre, Burg Platz (In der Burg)

wedding of the heir to the throne, Joseph II. Pacassi was also given the job of renovating the Court Library, because the domed building had settled dangerously due to weak foundations. From 1769, Pacassi also focused on the completion of Joseph's Square, which was finally finished by Franz Anton Hillebrand in 1776. This strictly symmetrical square is considered one of the loveliest in Vienna. In order to provide additional space for the Court Library, the Augustinian Wing was added on the southeast, concealing the Church of the Augustinian Friars behind its façade. Under Empress Maria Theresa the Hofapotheke (Imperial Court Pharmacy) was installed in the Stallburg. The art collection that had been housed there by Emperor Charles VI was moved to the Obere Belvedere (Upper Belvedere Palace) in 1776. The remaining towers of the old fortress were torn down (the south tower had previously been demolished by Joseph I). Two stairways were built (the Botschafterstiege and the Säulenstiege, the Ambassador's and Pillar Staircases, respectively). Because a Swiss Guard kept watch at the gateway to the oldest part of the Hofburg from 1748 to 1767, the names Schweizerhof (Swiss Court) and Schweizertrakt (Swiss Wing) have been used ever since. Joseph II (1741–1790) opened the Augarten and the Prater to the public and shifted the focus of new construction from his residence to public facilities, such as the Allgemeines Krankenhaus (General Hospital). His apartments in the Leopoldine Wing were furnished with far less magnificence than those of his mother, which were parallel to them. Here he built the "Controllorgang" (Inspector's Corridor) and held his audiences, which were open to the public, on the mezzanine floor.

The Congress of Vienna and the Gardens

Leopold II (1747–1792), who reigned for only two years, was succeeded by his son Francis II (1768–1835). Francis gave Tarouca Palace, to the south of the Augustinian monastery, to Albert, Duke of Saxe-Teschen, and his wife, Marie Christine, Maria Theresa's favorite daughter. Starting in 1800, it was remodeled by Louis Montoyer and, with the addition of a new wing, became what is today the Albertina. Responding to the coronation of Napoleon as emperor in 1804, Francis II elevated Austria to the status of an empire and, as Francis I, he became the first Austrian emperor. In 1806, after being defeated by Napoleon, who dictated the

Mid-19th century (steel engraving by J. M. Kolb): the Hofburg with the Montoyer Wing

dissolution of the Holy Roman Empire, Francis abdicated his title. The Empire, which had more than a thousand years of history as a multinational Christian realm, ceased to exist. In 1807 an equestrian statue of Joseph II was unveiled on the former Tummelplatz (Exercise Ground), which was renamed Josefsplatz (Joseph's Square). Between 1805 and 1807 Montoyer built a ceremonial wing that was called disparagingly "the nose" because it was added piecemeal to the Widmer Gate on the side facing the suburbs. Napoleon occupied Vienna on May 13, 1809, and after concluding a peace treaty with the Austrians on October 14, he blew up the fortifications in front of the Hofburg.

In October 1813, Napoleon was defeated in the Battle of the Nations at Leipzig. The Congress of Vienna, which convened from 1814 to 1815 and established a new European order, was a magnificent event. According to a contemporary bon mot, it didn't meet, it danced. Among those residing in the Hofburg were Tsar Alexander, King Frederick William of Prussia and King Frederick VI of Denmark. Napoleon was banished and peace was restored. Between 1816 and 1819, the remains of the Burg Bastion and the Spanish Bastion as well as the old Burgtor (Castle Gate) were torn down, the glacis was leveled, and the Volksgarten was laid out. Between 1819 and 1823 Pietro Nobile built the Temple of Theseus and the Cortisches Kaffeehaus in the Volksgarten. During the same period, the new monumental gateway of the Äusseres Burgtor was built (begun by Luigi Cagnola in 1821 and completed in 1824 by Nobile). In the Neuer k. u. k. Hofgarten (New Imperial and Royal Court Garden, called the Burggarten since 1919), Louis von Remy built two greenhouses of iron and glass (1818–1820 and 1823–1826, respectively). They immediately became the "attractions" of the Biedermeier period.

Francis II/I died in 1835 and was succeeded by his eldest son, Ferdinand I (1793–1875), who had no descendants. He commissioned a grand monument to his father, which was built between 1842 and 1846 on the square In der Burg, which was renamed Franzensplatz (Francis Square), the name it kept until 1918. In March 1848, the Parisian February Revolution spread to Vienna. Although the dreaded chancellor Prince Clemens Lothar Metternich was forced to resign by Ferdinand, crowds of people rose up and stormed the Stallburg, where the National Guard was quartered. Austria's first legislature met in the Winterreitschule (Winter Riding Hall). At the end of October, the situation escalated when Prince Alfred Windisch-Graetz brought his troops into position to retake Vienna. During three days of fighting, which was concentrated around the outer square of the Hofburg (now Heldenplatz) and the Burgtor gateway, a fire broke out in the attic of the Court Library.

Ferdinand I abdicated on December 2, 1848, and his brother, Archduke Francis Charles, renounced the throne in favor of his 18-year-old son, who was to reign for almost 68 years. Francis Joseph (1830–1916), who continued the conservative policies of his predecessors, was confronted with the rising national aspirations of his multinational monarchy. In 1867

October 1848: the roof of the Court Library (Augustinian and State Hall Wings) is set on fire during the civil war

Shortly before its demolition in 1888: the Court Theatre (Rudolf von Alt)

a "compromise" was reached with Hungary, resulting in the founding of the *österreichisch-ungarische Doppelmonarchie*, the "imperial and royal Dual Monarchy," which gave the Hungarians a high degree of independence.

The appearance of the Hofburg changed decisively for a final time under Francis Joseph. First, between 1850 and 1854, the Imperial Stables were remodeled and expanded by Leopold Mayer according to the original plans of Fischer von Erlach. The Winter Riding Hall in the Classicist style was added, and later, at the end of the 19th century, an octagonal pony riding hall was built at the request of Empress Elisabeth, who had married Francis Joseph in 1854.

The Dream of the Imperial Forum

At the end of 1857, Francis Joseph ordered the demolition of the city wall, which had long since lost any military significance. This cleared the way for construction on the glacis. The Ringstrasse (Ring Road) was created – four kilometers (2.5 miles) long, 57 meters (187 feet) wide and flanked by chestnut trees – along with its monumental buildings and palaces. In 1862, the architect Ludwig Förster proposed building the Court Museums instead of purely utilitarian buildings in the area between the Hofburg and the Imperial Stables. In 1864, Francis Joseph gave his approval. These buildings were to become the Kunsthistorisches and the Naturhistorisches Museums (museums of art and natural history, respectively). On the outer square (now Heldenplatz) an equestrian statue of Archduke Charles was unveiled in 1860. He had vanquished Napoleon at the Battle of Aspern in May 1809 (and been defeated by him at the Battle of Wagram in July). Five years later it was joined by a monument to Prince Eugene of Savoy, who had defeated the Turks in the 17ᵗʰ century, and the area became Heldenplatz (officially, only in 1918). The architectural competition for the new museum buildings, however, had not produced an acceptable submission.

In 1869, Gottfried Semper was persuaded to develop a concept for a Kaisersforum (Imperial Forum), but at the request of the Emperor, he had to base his design on an existing project. This resulted in an involuntary and anything-but-frictionless collaboration with Carl von Hasenauer. The new plan, which was submitted in the same year (and altered in 1871), provided for a throne-room building in front of the Leopoldine Wing. It had two large, curved wings projecting at right angles from a central "nose" and was to be connected with the two museums by buildings similar to triumphal arches across the Ring. In 1871, excavation work on the museums began. In 1881, Francis Joseph approved construction of the "Kaisergartenflügel" ("Imperial Garden Wing": the Neue Burg), but construction proved to be laborious and costly because it required excavating 25 meters (82 feet) down. In 1889 the Naturhistorisches Museum opened, and two years later the Kunsthistorisches Museum followed. There were also changes on the side of the Hofburg facing the city centre. In 1888 the old Hoftheater (Court Theatre)

The Imperial Forum designed by Gottfried Semper and Carl von Hasenauer in 1869

was torn down after the new Burgtheater by Semper and Hasenauer had been completed on the former Löwel Bastion. The concave Michaelertrakt (Michael's Wing) originally planned by Joseph Emanuel Fischer von Erlach could now be completed by Ferdinand Kirschner (following lengthy discussions about whether it should be topped with a dome). The cycle of statues by Lorenzo Mattielli on the façade of the Chancellery was extended with four additional "Labors of Hercules" beside the arched passageway, and by 1893 the Hofburg finally had a magnificent, showy façade. In 1898, the year that marked the 50th anniversary of Francis Joseph's reign, the Neue Burg was still under construction. In 1901 the old greenhouses were torn down and replaced with an Orangerie with Jugendstil elements according to plans by Friedrich Ohmann (completed in 1910). On the Ring, the Corps de Logis, which now houses the Museum of Ethnology, was finished in 1907, completing the Hofburg's new wing.

With the assassination of his wife, Elisabeth, in Geneva in 1898, the Emperor had lost interest in the protracted construction project. In 1906 the heir to the throne, Francis Ferdinand Archduke of Austria-Este, assumed responsibility and soon spoke out against construction of the throne-room building. In 1910 a much smaller Festival Hall Wing was built instead, connecting the Ceremonial Hall with the Neue Burg. In addition, plans for a second wing were abandoned, and a plan to substitute a colonnade was finally dropped as well. Thus the Imperial Forum envisioned by Semper and Hasenauer was to remain forever incomplete. In 1914, following the assassination of Francis Ferdinand in Sarajevo, World War I broke out. In November 1916, Francis Joseph died and was succeeded by his great nephew Charles (1887–1922). With the conclusion of World War I, the Austro-Hungarian monarchy came to an end, and the First Republic was proclaimed on November 11, 1918. Because Charles renounced governmental power but not the throne, he was forced with his family into exile.

The First Republic and the Nazi Period

In 1920 the Office of the Federal President was instituted as the highest office in the Republic of Austria. Some of the buildings in the Hofburg complex lost their usefulness, and many government employees had to be dismissed. Work to complete the interiors of the Festival Hall Wing and the

Neue Burg took until 1923 and 1926, respectively. In 1920, performances resumed at the Court Riding School. In 1921, the Wiener Messe GmbH (Vienna Exhibition and Fair Corporation) began using the Imperial Stables as exhibition space. Since 1922, the complex has been known as the Messepalast (Exhibition Palace). In 1928, the Museum of Ethnology, until that time housed in the Naturhistorisches Museum, opened in the Corps de Logis. In 1935, the Kunsthistorisches Museum's Collection of Arms and Armour moved into the Neue Burg.

DER ADLER DES HELDENDENKMALS

In 1933 and 1934, at the time of the corporative state, the Äusseres Burgtor was redesigned by Rudolf Wondraček and became the Heldendenkmal (Heroes' Monument) to the Victims of World War I. In 1935, gateways with eagle sculptures by Wilhelm Frass were added on the left and right. On March 15, 1938, four days after the invasion of Austria by German troops, Adolf Hitler announced from the balcony of the Neue Burg the annexation of Austria by the German Reich. Some 250,000 people turned out to cheer the Führer on Heldenplatz. The National Socialists planned to redesign the square and convert it into a parade ground, aligned parallel to the Ring and facing the Neue Burg. They never got that far: towards the end of World War II, Heldenplatz, which had been excavated in the autumn of 1943 to create a pond for supplying water to firefighters, was being used for farming. Between 1940 and 1945 the Messepalast was used by the Nazi regime for staging propaganda events.

Four days after the German invasion: Hitler on Heroes' Square on March 15, 1938

Ortner+Ortner's 1990 design for the MuseumsQuartier (above) and the one on which construction finally began in 1998 (below)

Reconstruction and the MuseumsQuartier

Allied bombing severely damaged not only the Stallburg, the Church of the Augustinian Friars and the Albertina but also the Offices of the Federal President in what is now the Federal Chancellery. In 1946, Karl Renner, who had been elected in December 1945 to be the first Federal President of the Second Republic, got approval from the Russians to move the President's Offices to the former living quarters of Maria Theresa and Joseph II in the Leopoldine Wing. From 1945 to 1955, the Neue Burg was the seat of the Inter-Allied Commission (symbolized to the Viennese by "four [nationalities riding together] in a Jeep"). In 1946 the Vienna Exhibition and Fair Corporation resumed its activities and subsequently built two large halls in the main courtyard of the Messepalast. The Hofburg was repaired and the Stallburg rebuilt. In 1955, following the signing of the Austrian State Treaty, the Lipizzaner horses returned to Vienna. In 1958, the Congress Centre was established in the Festival Hall Wing, and between 1962 and 1966 the Modern Library of the Austrian

National Library was installed in the Neue Burg.

In 1977, using the Imperial Stables to expand the capacity of the neighboring federal museums was considered for the first time. In 1983, it was decided to use the complex as a cultural forum, and in 1986 a two-stage architectural competition was announced. In 1989, Science Minister Erhard Busek (of the Austrian People's Party) referred to the site for the first time as the "MuseumsQuartier," setting the emphasis on contemporary art and culture. The jury recommended unanimously that the design by Laurids and Manfred Ortner be realized. It included two towers (a slender one with an elliptical ground-plan for the library and a cylindrical one for offices). But only a few weeks later, during the summer of 1990, a citizens' action group was formed, and in 1992 the populist newspaper *Kronen Zeitung* launched a campaign against the MuseumsQuartier project. As a result, it had to be downsized several times.

In the early hours of November 27, 1992, a fire broke out in the attic above the Redoutensäle, and the Large Hall was completely destroyed, although firefighters were able to prevent the flames from spreading to other wings. The attic was later converted to usable space. The Kleiner (Small) Redoutensaal was restored; the Grosser (Large) Redoutensaal was renovated and decorated with paintings by Josef Mikl. It reopened on October 26, 1997.

In December 1997 ground was broken for the Museums-Quartier, and in April 1998 construction began. In January 2001 the new buildings were handed over to their future tenants. The official opening of the grounds took place at the end of June. In September 2001 the Museum of Modern Art and the Leopold Museum opened. The renovation of the old buildings was completed in September 2002. Meanwhile in the autumn of 1999, renovation began on the Albertina, which had been closed since the mid-1990s. The museum was given a new study building, two exhibition halls and an underground storage area and reopened in March 2003. At the end of the year Hans Hollein's titanium roof projection was added to the building on the Augustinian Bastion.

Museum of Modern Art in June 2001:
a multimedia show to open the MQ

A Tour of the Grounds

In order to facilitate understanding of the complex architectural history of the Hofburg, the tour is organized chronologically. It begins in the oldest part of the complex, the Alte Burg (Old Castle). Today it is called the Schweizertrakt (Swiss Wing), because the Swiss Guard kept watch here for almost two decades, starting in 1748. Francis I Stephen of Lorraine, the husband of Empress Maria Theresa, had brought the Guard with him from Italy.

1st Loop:
The Middle Ages and the Renaissance

The core of the medieval Herzogsburg (Ducal Castle), which was probably founded by Otakar II Přemysl of Bohemia, was built between the 13th and 15th centuries. The stone fountain next to the gateway is decorated with a double-eagle relief in honor of a visit by Emperor Charles V in 1552. The Gothic ➤ **Hofburg Chapel** in the southern corner was consecrated in 1449. The ground-floor arcades and the Renaissance shape of the windows on the two main floors are the result of remodeling in the 1550s. The Säulenstiege (Pillar Staircase) in the northeast (like the Botschafterstiege – Ambassador's Staircase – on the opposite side) were built by Jean-Nicolas Jadot in the mid-18th century (it is worth having a look in the stairwell). This wing housed the apartments of Emperor Francis II/I (today it houses the Austrian Federal Office for the Care of Monuments). The Ecclesiastical and Secular ➤ **Schatzkammer (Treasury)** is located in the southeastern and northeastern wings.

A passageway on the southeast takes us across the Kapellenhof (Chapel Courtyard), where the chapel's choir, which was added later, is the only visible part of the façade, and on to Josefsplatz (Joseph's Square). This narrow courtyard was created in the second half of the 18th century when the moat was covered over. Joseph's Square was once the Exercise Ground. In the southeastern corner, hidden behind the Augustinian Wing of the Austrian

In the Swiss Court:
fountain with double eagle

National Library, is the ➤ **Augustinian Church,** built in the mid-14th century in Gothic style. We turn to the left (to the northeast) and come to the second large palace, the Stallburg, which was built in 1559 as a residence for Maximilian II. In 1565, the Emperor converted it into stables for his Spanish horses. The Stallburg, which is still the residence of the Lipizzaner horses today, is one of the few remaining Renaissance buildings in Vienna. The exterior façades have retained their original structure (apart from the enlarged windows on the ground floor). Because of the archway leading to the Winterreitschule (Winter Riding Hall), the entrance façade has lost the architectural effect it once had. The Hofapotheke (Imperial Court Pharmacy) was installed in the northern corner of the Stallburg in 1746. Today these rooms house the ➤ **Lipizzaner Museum.** The courtyard of the Stallburg is surrounded by a three-storey arcade with pilasters. The round fountain inscribed with the year 1675

Orientation maps of the Hofburg are posted throughout the grounds. The point of departure for the tour depicted here is the Swiss Court.

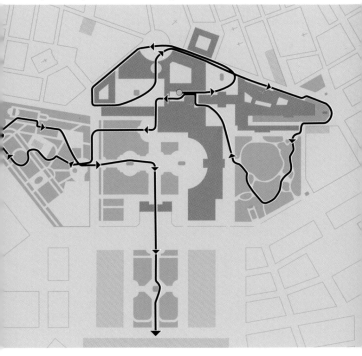

One of the few remaining Renaissance buildings in Vienna: the Stallburg with its arcaded courtyard

was originally in the Amalienburg (Amalia Residence). And that is where we go next: we head north on Reitschulgasse until we reach Michaelerplatz. In the middle of the square we can see excavated foundations from Roman times (2nd to 5th century) and of the first Ballhaus (Real Tennis Court, about 1530). This was the location of the original pleasure garden of the Hofburg, the Paradeisgartl. We turn to the northwest and walk down Schauflergasse.

On the left is the façade of the Imperial Chancellery Wing. It was built between 1723 and 1725 but is mentioned at this point because the Baroque façade with its bull's-eye panes bears the unmistakable signature of Johann Lucas von Hildebrandt. The last building on the right before we reach Bruno-Kreisky-Gasse is a Postmodern building (1982–1986) housing offices of the Foreign and Interior Ministries and the Federal Chancellery. In the mid-16th century, a hospital stood here and, after 1740, the new Imperial Ballhaus that gave the square its name. In media parlance, "Ballhausplatz" is used as a synonym for the Austrian government, much like "the White House" or "Downing Street." The **Federal Chancellery** (➤ **Environs**) was formerly the Geheime Hof- und Staatskanzlei (Secret Court and State Chancellery) and was built between 1717 and 1721 by Johann Lucas von Hildebrandt. The Court Hospital and the Ballhaus were torn down in 1903.

The Amalienburg is directly across from the Federal Chancellery. Construction began in 1575 and was completed by Pietro Ferrabosco in 1611. This Renaissance building, which Maximilian II built for his son Rudolf II, got its name in the first half of the 18th century when Empress Amalia, the widow of Joseph I, resided here. The irregular, four-winged complex has clean and simple façades with broad rustic work. The trapezoidal courtyard has a walled-up pergola and a simple Renaissance well.

The Leopoldine Wing adjoins the Amalienburg on the south, and we will discuss it presently. We walk through the flying buttress that connects the two buildings and back into the courtyard. This square, where tournaments were once held, is now called In der Burg. The façade of the Amalienburg is crowned by an octagonal tower with an early-Baroque helm roof. The lunar clock is said to have been designed by Tycho de Brahe, the court astronomer of Rudolf II. The apartments of Empress Elisabeth (➤ **Imperial Apartments**) are on the second floor (bel étage).

In 1552, two decades before construction of the Amalienburg began, the Schweizertor (Swiss Gate) of the Alte Burg was built by Pietro Ferrabosco at the opposite end of the square. This magnificent Renaissance portal still bears traces of the medieval fortress: for example, the winch for the chains of the drawbridge on either side of

the gate. The inscription names Ferdinand I with his official titles (Roman and German King, King of Hungary and Bohemia, Spanish Infante, Archduke of Austria and Duke of Burgundy). The coat of arms is edged with the chain of the Order of the Golden Fleece and shows a one-headed eagle because Ferdinand was not yet emperor at the time.

The Swiss Gate: built in 1552
by Pietro Ferrabosco

Baroque show of imperial power: the façade of the Imperial Chancellery Wing

2nd Loop:
The Baroque Period and Classicism

For almost a century, the four great corner pillars of the
Hofburg (Swiss Wing, Church of the Augustinian Friars,
Stallburg and Amalienburg) stood separately without a
wing to connect them. Only in 1660 did Leopold I decide
to extend the Alte Burg to the southwest with a wing
towards the Amalienburg. The Leopoldinische Trakt
(Leopoldine Wing), under which the imperial wine cellar
had been built, caught fire in 1668 only a few months
after its completion. Restoration work by Giovanni Pietro
Tencala was completed in 1681. The early-Baroque façade
extends without accentuation across 29 sets of windows
and was deliberately designed to conform to the façade of
the Alte Burg. Since 1946 the Leopoldine Wing has been
the office of the Austrian Federal President ➤ **Präsidentschaftskanzlei (Presidential Offices)**. The suite of
rooms on the second floor (bel étage) facing the courtyard
was the apartment of Empress Maria Theresa.

Much new construction occurred under Charles VI. First
the Emperor commissioned Johann Bernhard Fischer von
Erlach to build the Imperial Stables (1719–1725) and the
Court Library (1722–1730), which we will be discussing

later. Then Fischer's son, Joseph Emanuel, was entrusted with the Court Riding School (1729–1734) and the Michaelertrakt (Michael's Wing, (1728–1735) and was also commissioned to complete the Imperial Chancellery Wing, which Johann Lucas von Hildebrandt had begun on Schauflergasse in 1723. The façade on the courtyard side is magnificent and ostentatious. The central projection is topped with the coat of arms of Charles VI, with the imperial crown above it, surrounded by the personified virtues of the ruler. The pairs of sculptures on the side portals are by Lorenzo Mattielli: "Hercules and the Cretan Bull" and "Hercules and the Nemean Lion" on the northwest portal, "Hercules and Busiris" and "Hercules and Antaeus" on the southeast.

In addition to the police and the judicial administration of the Court, the Imperial Chancellery Wing housed the Imperial Court and State Archive from 1806 to 1902 as well as the most important of all Court offices, the Obersthofmeisteramt (Office of the Steward of the Household) with the ceremonial department. Following the dissolution of the Holy Roman Empire in 1806, part of the original chancellery rooms were converted into imperial apartments in which Emperor Francis Joseph later lived (➤ **Imperial Apartments**). On the ground floor is the former Court Porcelain and ➤ **Silver Collection**.

The monument to Emperor Francis II/I in the inner courtyard was created by Pompeo Marchesi between 1843 and 1846 on a commission from Ferdinand I in memory of his father. It was produced at the Manfredini bronze foundry in Milan and brought to Vienna in 33 days, drawn by eight pairs of oxen and nine pairs of horses. The four statues that surround the monument symbolize Faith (cross and star), Strength (lion's shield and club), Peace (sword and olive branch) and Justice (scales and sword). The Emperor is portrayed as Caesar Augustus in Roman robes. On the sides of the octagonal column are reliefs that depict the activities and qualities of the people (trade and commerce, mining and metallurgy, farming and stock-breeding, science, art and heroism). The inscription "Amorem meum populis meis" (To My People My Love) is taken from the last will and testament of Francis II/I. We now walk through the Kaisertor (Emperor's Gate) at the eastern corner of the square to reach Michaelerplatz (St. Michael's Square). On the left we see the **Loos-Haus** built between 1909 and 1911; on the right, the Gothic

Michaelerkirche (St. Michael's Church) with its Classicist façade (➤ **Environs**). We really should have approached this area from **Kohlmarkt** (➤ **Environs**) in order to get the full effect of the façade of Michaelertrakt (Michael's Wing) with its mighty dome. The concave semicircular façade with its sweeping, convex corners closes the Hofburg off from the city center. Construction of this wing began in 1728 but was interrupted in 1735, and for the next 150 years it remained a picturesque torso, reminiscent of an ancient ruin. The original plan of Joseph Emanuel Fischer was completed in 1893 by Ferdinand Kirschner. The central area of the façade is like a triumphal arch with a central projection flanked by double columns. The sculptural decoration is completed by two

The Cellars of the Hofburg

In the old days it was allegedly possible to traverse the cellars of the Hofburg from the Albertina to the Secret Chancellery – today the Federal Chancellery – and from the Court Riding School across the Schweizertrakt (Swiss Wing) and the "Segmentgang" (Segment Corridor) of the Neue Burg to the Kunsthistorisches Museum. The giant subterranean depot of the Austrian National Library has blocked some of the passageways, but this underground labyrinth remains huge. Without a guide from the security service, one would undoubtedly lose one's way. Unfortunately, the cellar levels – meaning the first and second levels – are as a rule not open to the public. The wine cellar used to be in the Leopoldine Wing, near the connecting corridor to the Chancellery (which in February 2000 had to be used by officials because of demonstrations against Austria's new right-wing government). Following the downfall of the monarchy, thousands upon thousands of bottles of wine, spirits and Champagne that had been stored there were auctioned off for the benefit of war victims. Only a giant oak barrel and a magnificent tiled tank that holds an unbelievable 731.5 hectoliters remind us of the cellars' former purpose. Now hundreds of plaster models of statues, monuments and reliefs are stored here, including horses and angels, a massive head of Goethe and a Jesus on the Cross, a massive imperial crown and numerous double eagles. The white statues look, as the author Gerhard Roth wrote in his essay *Die zweite Stadt* ("The Second City"), "… like the props of a dream that are designed to haunt the minds of the dead emperors." And together with the eerie monumental fountains (on the left: "Austria, Ruler of the Sea" by Rudolf Weyer; on the right: Edmund von Hellmer's "Austria, Ruler of the Land"). The cycle of statues begun on the Imperial Chancellery Wing continues on either side of the gateway with four more "Labors of Hercules." The pediment is crowned with allegories of Wisdom, Justice and Power. Above the central gateway arcade is the coat of arms of Habsburg-Austria-Lorraine with trombone-playing figures on either side. Behind the façade of the left-hand wing lies the ➤ **Spanish Riding School**. The Winterreitschule (Winter Riding Hall), built by Joseph Emanuel Fischer between 1729 and 1734, fills the entire building along Reitschulgasse.

We now head down that street in a southerly direction.

In the cellars of the Leopoldine Wing: hundred of plaster models of statues, monuments and reliefs

vaulting, they provide an impressive setting for whodunits (for example, Austrian television's *Kommissar Rex*).

Heading towards the south, before we reach the semicircular choir of the Burgkapelle (Hofburg Chapel), we pass the old Zentralkesselhaus (Central Boiler Room), which in 1953 was converted into a coal-fired central heating plant for the complex but was taken out of service long ago, and the former ice cellar. Ice taken from the Danube was emptied through trap-doors in the barrel vaulting into two rooms that were a good eight meters (26 feet) high. There were semispherical metal humps in the floor, and food was stored directly beneath them.

Beyond the passageway we arrive again at Josefsplatz (Joseph's Square), one whole side of which is occupied by the originally free-standing Court Library (1722–1726), built on plans by Johann Bernhard Fischer. Its ➤ **Prunk-saal (State Hall)** consists of two naves and a large main hall, the central projection of which dominates the entire structure. The sculptural decorations are restricted to the attic zone. In the middle is Pallas Athena (Lorenzo Mattielli, around 1725), who is driving out Envy and Ignorance with her four-in-hand chariot. The atlases on either side are by Hans Gasser (around 1865). On the left they depict Atlas with the Celestial Sphere as well as Astronomy and Astrology, the Allegories of Astronomy; on the right we see Gaea with the Terrestrial Globe as well as Geometry and Geography, the Allegories of Metrology. In the mid-18th century Empress Maria Theresa commissioned Jean-Nicolas Jadot to convert the former Komödiensaal (Theatre) on the northeastern side of Joseph's Square into two ballrooms, the ➤ **Redoutensäle**. Nikolaus Pacassi began plans for the final architectural completion of the square in 1769, and by 1776 an apparently strictly symmetrical Ehrenhof (Court of Honor) had been built. The façades of the Augustinian and Redoutensaal Wings match the strict architectural design of the Court Library. The bronze equestrian monument to Emperor Joseph II, which was commissioned by Francis II/I, was made by Franz Anton Zauner (1795–1807). As can be seen from the clothing and footwear of the Emperor, it was inspired by the statue of Marcus Aurelius at the Capitol in Rome. Two palaces form the fourth side of Josefsplatz. The early-Classicist façade of Palavicini Palace (No. 5), which was built by Johann Ferdinand Hetzendorf (1783/1784), caused a scandal because of its revolutionary simplicity. Palffy Palace (No. 6), which underwent extensive alterations in 1956, was built in around 1575. The Classicist elements of the façade date from 1800.

We now walk down Augustinerstrasse past the Church and Monastery of the Augustinians to Lobkowitzplatz with the ➤ **Österreichisches Theatermuseum (Austrian Theatre Museum)** on the left and continue to the _ Albertina, which is also the home of the ➤ **Film Museum**. In around 1745, Emanuel Teles Count Sylva-Tarouca built a three-storey palace on the Bastion, which was 11 meters (36 feet) above street level. On a commission from Albert, Duke of Saxe-Teschen, Louis Montoyer began

Soaring into the square: Hans Hollein's flying roof for the Albertina

remodeling work in 1800, expanding the palace to the southwest with a wing that had a long, twenty-window façade. The projecting flying roof on the Bastion as well as the stairs were built between 2001 and 2003 in the course of the renovation and expansion of the Albertina on plans by Hans Hollein. He is also responsible for the Postmodern base zone with its bull's-eye windows on Augustinerstrasse. They make it clear that the two cellar basement levels of the palace were previously not exposed: a long ramp was torn down after World War II and replaced by a flight of steps.

On Albertinaplatz stands Alfred Hrdlicka's 1988 **Monument Against War and Fascism** (➤ **Environs**). The south-easternmost point of the Hofburg is the Danubiusbrunnen (Danube Fountain, 1864–1869), based on a design by Moritz von Löhr. Johann Meixner's figures in white Carrara marble are found in the nine – originally eleven – niches of the Augustinerbastei (Augustinian Bastion). They symbolize rivers, including the Danube, Mur, Salzach, March, Raab and Enns. On the Bastion stands a bronze equestrian statue of the Austrian field marshal Archduke Albert. It was made by Caspar von Zumbusch in 1899.

To the southeast we see the back of the **State Opera** (➤ **Environs**). We walk around the fountain in a clock-wise direction and turn right on Hanuschgasse. From there a ramp leads up to the Albertina. We continue, how-ever, through the Abrahamtor (Abraham's Gate) with the simple stone statue of the preacher Abraham a Santa

Built by Friedrich Ohmann in Jugendstil: the Palmenhaus

Clara, made in 1928 by Hans Schwarthe, and into the Burggarten. This garden was laid out between 1817 and 1819 after the Burg Bastion had been demolished by the French (1809) and the fortifications had been torn down. Until the downfall of the monarchy in 1918, it was reserved for the use of the imperial family. Francis I, who loved gardens and flowers, is said to have been personally involved in details of the planning. The garden had to be downsized on the northeast to make room for the monumental Neue Burg in 1881. In addition, the old glasshouses had to be torn down, and between 1902 and 1906 Friedrich Ohmann replaced them with the Jugendstil structure of the Palmenhaus (on the northwest, parallel to the Albertina). Today it houses a café-restaurant and the ➤ **Schmetterlinghaus** (**Butterfly House**).

In the southern corner stands a bronze statue of Emperor Francis Joseph. The monument on the southwest to Wolfgang Amadeus Mozart, made in 1896 by Viktor Tilgner,

originally stood on Albertinaplatz, which was called Albrechtsplatz (Albert's Square) at the time, in front of the present Café Mozart. It was taken to safety after the bombing on March 12, 1945, and moved to the Burggarten in June 1953. The bas relief on the front depicts the invitation of the Stone Guest (Commenda-

In the Burggarten only since 1953: the Mozart Monument

tore) in the opera *Don Giovanni*. On the back is the six-year-old composer at the piano with his sister, Nannerl, and his father, Leopold, with his violin. On the west side of the garden, towards the Neue Burg, stands an equestrian statue of Francis I Stephen of Lorraine. Work on this monument in early-Classicist style by Balthasar Ferdinand Moll was begun during the Emperor's lifetime. It was first placed in the new Paradeisgartl on the Burg Bastion in 1797; in 1819 it was moved to the Kaisergarten.

A path leads to the north between the Neue Burg and the Palmenhaus to the Bibliothekshof (Library Courtyard), where we can see the rear façade of the former Court Library with the ➤ **Prunksaal (State Hall)**. In the northern corner of the so-called Verbindungstrakt (Connecting Wing), an inconspicuous passageway leads to the Kapellenhof (Chapel Courtyard) and from there we can re-enter the Schweizerhof (Swiss Court) and continue back to the inner courtyard (In der Burg). We now turn left and walk through the former Widmer Gate towards Heldenplatz (Heroes' Square). On the right, at the beginning of the pedestrian arcade, we see the exposed stonework of the medieval Widmerturm (Widmer Tower), which was torn down in 1753. The second part of the arcade is the Montoyer Wing, which used to be called the "Nase" (nose). The building, which used to project from the Leopoldine Wing into what is now Heldenplatz, was built by Louis Montoyer (1802–1806) and houses the Ceremonial Hall. Adjoining it is the Festival Hall Wing, built between 1910 and 1923 in the style of late historicism.

Heldenplatz and the Imperial Forum

We are now standing at the edge of Heldenplatz (Heroes' Square). On the far side is the Äusseres Burgtor. Its columned façade facing the Hofburg is an imitation of the Propylaeum in Athens. The building with its five arched gateways and two wings was built between 1821 and 1824 in the Classicist style. In 1934 it was redesigned as a ➤ **Heldendenkmal** (Heroes' Monument). After the destruction of the Burg Bastion, the huge area was intended to serve as a parade ground, but it was not completed until the early 20th century when the Neue Burg was built. Heldenplatz gets its name from the two monumental sculptures of heroes: on the northwest stands a monument to Archduke Charles, who defeated Napoleon

A reproduction of the one in Athens: The Temple of Theseus

at the Battle of Aspern in May 1809 and was defeated by him at Wagram in July. The outstanding equestrian statue made by Anton Dominik Fernkorn between 1853 and 1859 was unveiled in 1860. The monument to Prince Eugene of Savoy, the "Noble Knight" and commander to three emperors (Leopold I, Joseph I and Charles VI), was erected five years later on the southeast. The bronze equestrian statue (the Lipizzaner is executing the figure called a levade) on a pedestal of polished marble was begun by Fernkorn in 1860 and completed by Franz Pönninger. Instead of going straight ahead, we turn right towards the northwest. The façade of the Leopoldine Wing facing the suburbs is stepped and elaborately structured. The balcony was added in 1750 by Jean-Nicolas Jadot. Joseph II, a son of Maria Theresa, lived in the state rooms on this side. Since 1946 they have been part of the ➤ **Präsidentschafts-kanzlei (Presidential Offices)**. The projection on the narrow side was built in 1875 after the Bellaria ramp, which had been built to allow Empress Maria Theresa easy access to the second floor, was torn down.

We now walk across the Volksgarten (People's Park), to which we will return after the tour. In this area, where fortifications used to stand, Maria Theresa built the new Paradeisgartl atop the wall. After the destruction of the Burg Bastion, the park was laid out within the remaining city walls in 1819 and opened in 1823 as the exact counterpart of the private Kaisergarten (Imperial Garden). Instead of winding paths, the Court Architect Louis von Remy chose a strictly geometrical layout so as not to "open the way to indecency." This was part of efforts during the Biedermeier period – also called "Vormärz" (the period before the March 1848 revolution) – to allow the police to better monitor the Emperor's subjects. Between 1819 and 1823 Pietro Nobile built in the Volksgarten the ➤ **Temple of Theseus** – a smaller copy of the one in Athens – and the Cortisches Kaffeehaus with its semicircular colonnade. Expanded several times, it is now the ➤ **Volksgarten** Club Discothèque. Later a fountain with the "Triton and Nymph" bronze sculpture by Viktor Tilgner (1880) was added along with an octagonal water reservoir house (1890), which was converted in 1924 into the Meierei milk-bar.

Because the curtain wall that separated the park from the glacis had been torn down in 1860, it was now possible for the Hofburg complex to extend all the way to the new Ringstrasse. In this eastern area, which was laid out between 1863 and 1865, a central fountain by Anton Dominik Fernkorn was added in 1866. In 1889 a monument to Franz Grillparzer was unveiled (a larger-than-life seated figure by Carl Kundmann; the architectural design was by Carl von Hasenauer). The reliefs depict scenes from Grillparzer's dramas. Starting in 1884, the Volksgarten was extended towards Löwelstrasse. Since 1907 this area has been dominated by a monument to Empress Elisabeth with the remarkable Jugendstil architecture of Friedrich Ohmann (seated figure by Hans Bitterlich). Immediately behind it we see the **Burgtheater** (➤ **Environs**). In 1921 the bronze statue of a young athlete by Josef Müllner was placed in front of the Temple of Theseus. Next to the Volksgarten Restaurant, Oswald Haerdtl opened a "Milchbar" in 1951, a glass pavilion with a penthouse roof, still in its original condition.

After our tour through the park, we turn to the southeast and look across Heldenplatz to the historicist Neue Burg. This mighty structure with its curved façade is only one of two wings that were originally planned. In order to better understand the Imperial Forum project, which was based

With the Burgtheater in the background: the monument to Empress Elisabeth

The Imperial Forum was never finished: the Neue Burg with the Corps de Logis

on an 1860s concept, we go back to the street that runs
from Michaelerplatz through Widmer Gate to the
Äusseres Burgtor. It is the central axis of a gigantic symmetrical complex that is bounded on the southwest by the
Imperial Stables, where the MuseumsQuartier opened in
2001. Implementation of the plans by Gottfried Semper
and Carl von Hasenauer began in 1871. The first buildings outside the Ring were the Kunsthistorisches and the
Naturhistorisches Museums. In 1881 work also got
underway on the Kaisergartenflügel (Neue Burg), which
17 years later, on the 50th anniversary of the reign of
Emperor Francis Joseph I, had still not been completed. In
1906 the heir to the throne, Francis Ferdinand, opposed
the building of a domed "Throne Room Wing" because
of the cost involved. It would have been placed in front of
the Leopoldine Wing and the "nose." Instead, a smaller
Festival Hall Wing was built between 1910 and 1923 to
link the Montoyer Wing and Alte Burg with the Neue
Burg. Since 1958, it has served (along with other rooms)
as the ➤ **Hofburg Congress Centre**. In 1913, a year before
the outbreak of World War I, plans to build the opposite
wing in the Volksgarten were abandoned: the Imperial
Forum was to remain only a torso.
The Neue Burg consists of a mighty central projection
with two segmented wings, each with nine pairs of
columns. Between the windows of the lower storey are 20
sculptures, symbolically representing the history and peoples of Austria. From the balcony, Adolf Hitler announced
the annexation of Austria by the German Reich in March
1938. Access to the Modern Library of the ➤ **Österreichische Nationalbibliothek** as well as to three collections of

the Kunsthistorisches Museum: the ➤ **Hofjagd- und Rüst-kammer (Collection of Arms and Armour)**, the ➤ **Ephesus Museum** and the ➤ **Sammlung alter Musikinstrumente (Collection of Ancient Musical Instruments)** is through the portico. Adjoining the Neue Burg towards the Ringstrasse is the Corps de Logis, which was completed in 1907. With its impressive, glassed-in courtyard, it was intended to provide lodging for guests. Today it houses the photo archive and portrait collection of the Austrian National Library. Since 1928 it has also been the home of the ➤ **Museum of Ethnology**.

We now pass through the Äusseres Burgtor and head in the direction of the former Imperial Stables. From the Ring we can see that the central axis of the strictly symmetrical Kaiserforum (Imperial Forum) leads not only to the main entrance of the MuseumsQuartier but past the former Imperial Stables and on to the district of Spittelberg beyond. In the courtyard of the Stiftskaserne military base stands a cylindrical anti-aircraft tower of steel-reinforced concrete. It was built during World War II as one of six such emplacements in Vienna. After the war the "shooting cathedral," as it was euphemistically called by Hitler's architect Friedrich Tamm, was supposed to become a "Totenburg" ("Fortress of the Dead"), a giant mausoleum for the fallen soldiers. Tamm planned to cover the outermost edge, with its extended bastions, with black marble that had already been selected. His vision for this practically indestructible "hall of glory" was taken in part from Castel del Monte in Apulia.

We now cross the Ring to Maria Theresa Square. At the center is Anton Dominik von Fernkorn's monument to the Empress, which was unveiled in 1888. His pyramidal composition rises to a summit at her diadem. On the left is the ➤ **Kunsthistorisches Museum** (opened in 1891) and on the right the ➤ **Naturhistorisches Museum** (1889). They are mirror images of one another. Half columns provide structure to the central projection, and each has a large central dome and four satellite cupolas.

A mirror image of the Natural History Museum: the Museum of Art History

TOUR

Heldenplatz as an Historic Focal Point

No other event is so closely associated with Heldenplatz (Heroes' Square) as the seemingly endless cheering of the population there after German troops invaded and occupied Austria. On March 15, 1938, Adolf Hitler announced the annexation of Austria by the Third Reich from the balcony of the Neue Burg. In his play *Heldenplatz*, which caused an unbelievable commotion in Austria before and after the 1988 première at the Burgtheater, Thomas Bernhard (1931–1989) lets this cheering rise to an almost unbearable level.

Abused by the National Socialists, Heldenplatz has always been used for important state events, regardless of the political system, and for large events of all kinds (Catholic conferences, open-air concerts, festivals, sporting events as well as by the army for parades and swearing-in ceremonies). It is regarded as the focal point and nucleus of recent Austrian history with all its contradictions and competing ideologies, a symbol of both power and defeat, of both psychological repression and political protest.

The square was created in an act of humiliation: Napoleon blew up the Burg Bastion and the Spanish Bastion in 1809. The rubble was cleared away and the area leveled after the Congress of Vienna. Called the Paradeplatz until 1821, it was intended for military parades. In the revolutionary year of 1848, the area became a battlefield on which more than 2000 lives were lost. The name Heldenplatz has been used only since 1865 when the second equestrian statue was unveiled: Archduke Charles and Prince Eugene of Savoy were among the monarchy's most successful commanders.

Heldenplatz, which is open on the north and separated from the Volksgarten only by a railing, is also part of a torso, because the Neue Burg was never completed. Thus even though the megalomaniac plans for the Imperial Forum project had already been abandoned in 1913, the square stands for the fall of the Habsburg empire and the dissolution of the multinational state of Austria-Hungary. In 1925, there was a mass demonstration on Heldenplatz in favor of Austria being annexed by the German Reich. In 1931 there was a "Völkische Kundgebung" ("national demonstration") by the National Socialists, and in 1934 a demonstration for Chancellor Engelbert Dollfuss, who had been assassinated by illegal Nazi Party members after he had dissolved Parliament and established an authoritarian regime ("Austro-Fascism"). In 1935 there was a parade by the Ostmärkische Sturmscharen (a Catholic paramilitary organization) at which Chancellor Kurt Schuschnigg spoke (on the steps in front of the Neue Burg's balcony), and in the autumn of 1938 there was a large demonstration of the NSDAP (Nazi Party).

In February 1972, a huge crowd on Heldenplatz expressed its solidarity with the skier Karl Schranz, who had been excluded from participation in the Olympic Games for flimsy reasons. In September 1983, Pope John Paul II blessed Heldenplatz during a vesper service for Europe, and in June 1998, he said mass there. Nobel Peace laureate Elie Wiesel waved to the crowd from the "Hitler balcony" in June 1992 at a "Concert for Austria." In January 1993, 250,000 people holding burning candles ("The Sea of Lights") demonstrated against racism and a xenophobic petition sponsored by the rightwing, populist Freiheitliche Partei (Freedom Party). In February 2000 the crowd was demonstrating against the conservative People's Party's decision to enter into a coalition with the Freedomites. Meanwhile Heroes' Square has become the finish line of the Vienna Marathon and thus, perhaps, truly deserving of its name.

Thousands of burning candles to demonstrate against racism and xenophobia: the "Sea of Lights" on Heldenplatz in 1993

Dominating the skyline behind the MuseumsQuartier: the Nazi-era anti-aircraft tower at the Stiftskaserne military base in Spittelberg

The Imperial Stables and the MuseumsQuartier

The Imperial Stables, on which construction began in 1719, only appear to fit into the Imperial Forum, which is 150 years younger. They are not quite at a right angle to the axis between the two museums and the Neue Burg. Johann Bernhard Fischer von Erlach aligned his building with the old wing of the Hofburg Palace and not with Michaelerplatz (St. Michael's Square), as did the architects of the late 19th century. This cannot be seen from a distance, but for the architects of the MuseumsQuartier, Laurids and Manfred Ortner, this symmetric deviation was of great significance, as we shall see.

But first we approach the multi-axis façade. By giving the façade a rhythmical structure, Fischer von Erlach was somehow able to deal with its enormous size (a respectable 355 meters, 1129 feet). With their prominent central projection the Imperial Stables appear more like a palace than a utilitarian building. Fischer von Erlach's model, after all, was his reconstruction of Nero's palace in Rome, the Domus Aurea (Golden House). Nevertheless, there is a certain discrepancy between the width and the height of the two-storey building. During the war with Napoleon, the Imperial Stables were seriously damaged. In the course of renovation in 1815, two towers along the sides and the gable of the central building were demolished.

Between 1850 and 1854 other significant changes were made, especially to the interior of the complex. Leopold

Mayer enlarged the building, for the most part remaining true to Fischer von Erlach's design. But only the transverse wings were built in Neo-Baroque style. The central Winter Riding Hall clearly speaks the language of Classicism. Mayer changed the façade on the courtyard side of the old building, which used to be less ornamented. He inserted larger windows, added a balcony, and placed terraces between the staircases. In the course of the restoration in 2001, the building received a coat of salmon paint, similar to the color that the building is believed to have had during the Baroque period. If you cross into the courtyard, you will notice that some sections of the building are painted a lighter, yellow color, which is supposed to be that of 1854. The various nuances in the paint make it easy to recognize the period during which each part of the building was completed.

The Main Courtyard, which is the largest enclosed square in Vienna, is dominated by three free-standing buildings: in the center is the Winterreithalle (Winter Riding Hall), now the home of the two performance and event halls ➤ **Halls E + G.** Because this building was built at the same time as the Fischer von Erlach Wing, its central projection with the three-axis notched arcades and the horsehead shaped arch-stones is no longer oriented towards the axis of Michaelerplatz – Maria-Theresien-Platz. The ➤ **Leopold Museum** to the left of the Winter Riding Hall, however, is oriented parallel to the two Court Museums. Hence, it "docks" with the axis of the Imperial Forum. The outside surfaces, including the roof, are faced with white limestone. The interior structure of the building is evident on the façade as well: the walls of the rooms are indicated by slight grooves in the surface, creating an almost antique effect.

The ➤ **Museum of Modern Art,** a cube with a curved roof surface, is even more oriented towards the center of the square than the Leopold Museum. But this rotation was not an arbitrary decision either: the building reflects the structure of the Spittelberg. In contrast to the Leopold Museum, which is oriented towards imperial splendor, it points toward the bourgeois culture in which Modernism has its roots. The Museum with its curved roof, dark-gray basalt lava and narrow windows is in stark contrast to the Leopold Museum. It resembles a nearly impregnable fortress or a huge monolith that appears to have grown up from the ground. The size of the stone slabs, whose shading changes with the weather, increases towards the top, which lends the massive building a dynamic air. A small gap between the façade and the square provides an open view into the deep. The Museum had to be "pushed into the ground," according to the architectural theorist Friedrich Achleitner, so that the old silhouette would not be affected. Both museum buildings had to be repeatedly downsized in response to protests by preservationists. This also explains why they can hardly be seen from outside the complex: the height of the new buildings was not permitted to be greater than that of the central projection of the Fischer von Erlach Wing. It is especially sad that there is no outward sign – a tower or a column – to serve from afar as a symbol of contemporary architecture and of the MuseumsQuartier.

The third building by the brothers Ortner, the ➤ **Kunsthalle Wien,** is located behind the Winter Riding Hall and accessed through the latter. This municipal exhibition hall shares its foyer with the performance and event Halls E and G. The entrance area, a former gateway, was especially accentuated: it is lined with red clinker bricks, the surface material of the Kunsthalle. The two large museums can be approached via two open staircases on the left and right. Continuing across bridges, one can reach the finished attic of the Oval Wing, which is behind the Kunsthalle, and the entrance on Breite Gasse.

We continue our stroll on ground level, turn right, and walk through the Main Courtyard along the Fischer von Erlach Wing, in which we find the theme street Electric Avenue of ➤ **quartier21.** The second floor of the Baroque building was used by veterinarians, drivers, coachmen, blacksmiths, valets, stablemen, grooms, court servants, doorkeepers and stable masters. Through the gateway we reach the Staatsratshof (State Councilor's Courtyard) with the ➤ **Architekturzentrum Wien.** The event hall "Podium" was formerly the saddler's workshop; the information room of "basis wien" was formerly used for leather storage. We continue in a southeasterly direction and come to the Sattlerhof. Towards the end of the 19th century at the request of Empress Elisabeth, an octagonal riding hall was built, a half-timbered building with exposed brickwork. Today it houses the library of the Architekturzentrum. We turn left and pass a steep ramp, which leads to the Glacis-Beisl and continues in a semicircle to the second floor of the Neo-Baroque Imperial Stables.

Our path leads along the Museum of Modern Art to the rear entrance of the Kunsthalle. It was built as a free-standing building on the site of the open-air Summer Riding School. It stands close to the Winter Riding Hall, whose roof edge it overlaps with its brick roof. In contrast to the richly decorated edifice of the Winter Riding Hall, which was designed for purposes of traditional representation, the façade is reminiscent of a factory. On the other side of the "ravine" is the Oval Wing. The lateral wing, which adjoins it on the northeast, houses the ➤ **Tanzquartier Wien** on its upper floor.

We return to the Main Courtyard and see the southeastern wing of the Fischer von Erlach Wing with the theme street "transeuropa" of ➤ **quartier21**. The sculptural horse-heads on the portals of the building indicate its original use. Through one of the two gateways, we reach the Fürstenhof (Prince's Courtyard) with the ➤ **Zoom Kindermuseum** and the ➤ **Dschungel (Theatre for Young Audiences)**. Behind it is the Klosterhof (Cloister Courtyard). Today the former Klosterschule (Cloister School) is the studio of the TV station Puls TV. Another gateway leads to Mariahilfer Strasse. If you want a real overview of the complex, turn right and visit the cafeteria and roof terrace of the furniture store Leiner at Mariahilfer Strasse 18 (opening times: Mondays to Fridays 9:30 a.m. to 6:30 p.m., Saturdays 9 a.m. to 5 p.m.). The view, which takes in far more than just the MuseumsQuartier and the Hofburg, is impressive.

Evening rendezvous: the Main Courtyard of the MuseumsQuartier

Albertina

ADDRESS: Albertinaplatz 1
OPENING TIMES: daily 10 a.m. to 6 p.m., Wednesday until 9 p.m.
GUIDED TOURS: Saturday, Sunday and holidays at 3:30 p.m.
PHONE: +43/1/534 83 0
INTERNET: www.albertina.at, E-MAIL: info@albertina.at

Albrecht Dürer: "The Hare"
(watercolor, 1502)

The Albertina is the largest and most valuable collection of graphic arts in the world. At present it has around 65,000 drawings and almost a million graphic reproductions from the late Gothic to the contemporary modern period. The Albertina is generally associated with Albrecht Dürer's "Praying Hands" and "The Hare," but its collection of outstanding works ranges from Raphael, Michelangelo, Leonardo da Vinci, Rembrandt and Rubens to Eugène Delacroix, Edouard Manet and Paul Cézanne. In addition, the Albertina also has a large number of works by Egon Schiele, Gustav Klimt, Oskar Kokoschka, Pablo Picasso, Robert Rauschenberg and Anselm Kiefer.

The foundations were laid by the man who gave the Albertina its name: Albert Kasimir, Duke of Saxe-Teschen (1738–1822). Together with his wife, Marie Christine, the favorite daughter of Maria Theresa, he spent 50 years amassing his collection. In addition to the drawings and prints, there are two large special collections. The architectural collection consists of around 25,000 drawings, sketches and models, including a wealth of material from the estates of Francesco Borromini, Johann Bernhard Fischer von Erlach, Carl von Hasenauer, Adolf Loos and Clemens Holzmeister. The photographic collection, which was established in October 1999, contains the institution's own holdings as well as those of the Höhere Graphischen Bundes-Lehr- and Versuchsanstalt (Graphics School) in Vienna and the collection of the legendary publisher Langewiesche, famous for its photographic volumes *Die Blauen Bücher*, ("The Blue Books").

History: Around 1745, Emanuel Teles Graf Sylva-Tarouca, who was president of the Niederländische Kanzlei (Dutch Chancellery) and the Court Building Surveyor of Empress Maria Theresa, built a three-storey palace on the Augustinerbastei (Augustinian Bastion), which was 11 meters (36 feet) above street level. The trapezoidal outline of the foundations resulted from the previous building on the site, a mid-17ᵗʰ century storehouse for building materials.

Shortly before her death in 1780, Maria Theresa appointed the husband of Marie Christine – Albert, Duke of Saxe-Teschen – to be the new governor of the Austrian Netherlands. Albert initially gave up the use of his palace in Vienna and moved to Brussels, where he commissioned Charles de Wailly and Louis Montoyer to build Laeken Palace. In 1792, he and Marie Christine were forced by the Napoleonic Wars to flee Brussels. Emperor Francis II/I gave them Tarouca Palace and the adjoining part of the Augustinian monastery as a gift.

In 1800, two years after the death of his wife, the Duke commissioned Louis Montoyer to remodel it. First the Monastery Wing was modernized to provide a home for the Duke's growing collection of drawings and reproductions. In a second phase of construction, the palace was expanded, with a long wing with 20 sets of windows facing what is now the Burggarten.

At Albert's death in 1822, his heir was Archduke Charles, who had been adopted. He commissioned

The Albertina over the centuries: the palace of Count Sylva-Tarouca (c. 1800), the Danube Fountain (c. 1900) and the building after it was bombed in March 1945

Magnificent: the Gold Cabinet with
its Sèvres table

Josef Kornhäusel to completely rearrange the palace and decorate the rooms in the style of Classicism. The entrance to the *piano nobile* (floor above the ground floor) was now via the Minerva Hall, the Colonnade and the Sphinx Staircase. Next to the Festival Hall, which was divided into two rooms, a ballroom was built. Today it is the home of a cycle by Joseph Klieber: *Apollo and the Nine Muses*. Although all the rooms were newly decorated with paneling, wall lamps and trellises as well as wall coverings and window drapes, some furnishings were used that Albert had brought with him from Laeken Palace when he returned to Vienna.

At the death of Charles in 1847, ownership was transferred to his eldest son, Archduke Albert. Between 1864 and 1868, after the demolition of the fortifications, Moritz von Löhr redesigned what remained of the Bastion, creating the Albrechtsrampe (Albert's Ramp) and the Danubiusbrunnen (Danube Fountain). Johann Meixner created the allegoric river figures in Carrara marble for the 11 arched niches, now only nine. In 1899, the equestrian statue of Albert by Carl von Zumbusch was installed on the Bastion. In 1906 Archduke Frederick decided to add to the palace. This was still in planning when World War I broke out in 1914, and the project was abandoned. With the downfall of the monarchy, ownership of the palace was transferred to the new Republic. In 1920 the collection was combined with the graphics collection of the former Imperial Court Library, and in 1921 it was given the name Staatliche Graphische Sammlung Albertina (Albertina State Graphics Collection). In March 1945, just before the end of World War II, the palace and the bastion were severely damaged by bombing. In the course of restoration between 1948 and 1950, massive changes were made. Although it had not been hit by bombing, the long ramp was torn down and replaced with a stairway. The main entrance was moved from the Bastion to Augustinerstrasse, and much of the decoration on the façade of the palace was removed.

In the mid-1990s, the museum had to be closed for long-overdue renovation, which took longer than expected. In 1999, a study building with a library and workshops as well as a subterranean depot were built on the Burggarten side. The change is almost unnoticeable from the exterior. Director Klaus Albrecht Schröder was also able to garner support for building two exhibition halls and restoring parts of the Baroque façade to their condition of 1822 and 1867, respectively. Thus the entrance was moved back to the front of the palace on the Bastion and the courtyard was roofed over. The Albertina reopened in March 2003. The titanium roof project, named "Soravia Wing" for its sponsor, was completed in the autumn of 2003. The "wing" was the work of Hans Hollein, who also designed the Postmodern base zone on Augustinerstrasse with its bull's eye windows and wave relief.

Tour: Crossing the Harriet Hartmann Court, which is the box office and center of activity (the restaurant on the left, the shop on the right), we reach the oval Minerva Hall, dominated by a statue of the goddess. On the left, an escalator leads to the subterranean Bastei Hall, which

The ballroom on the *piano nobile* with the cycle *Apollo and the Nine Muses*

is mainly used for displaying contemporary art and photography. Behind Minerva Hall, the Colonnade with its artificial-marble columns leads to the Sphinx Staircase. The Pfeiler Hall to the left as well as the Studio Gallery below on the mezzanine level are used for small individual shows. Above the stairway with its two sphinxes, we come to the *piano nobile*. On the right is the Propter Homines Hall in the Augustinian Monastery Wing. In this area were once the collection of Archduke Albert and a Classicistic library corridor.

We proceed straight ahead to the State Rooms (including the Muses' Hall, Tea Salon, Billiards Room, Audience Chamber, Study and Spanish Apartment). They look as they did between 1822 and 1825, but most of the furnishings are considerably older (e.g. in the mirrored Golden Cabinet and the ceramic panels in the Wedgwood Room), because they came from Laeken Palace. The Rococo Room, however, dates from around 1870: Matilda, the daughter of Archduke Albert, was a secret smoker and set herself on fire – much like Paulinchen in the German fairytale – and the furnishings with her. Thus the walls are covered not in silk but in satin. The Kaminzimmer (Fireplace Room) was furnished in 1897.

The small Sèvres table in the Golden Cabinet (a gift from King Louis XVI and Marie-Antoinette) and the center chandelier in the Muses' Hall are the only original items remaining. They were later purchased from the heirs of Archduke Frederick, who after the expropriation of 1919 had received permission to take furniture, carpets, vases, mantle clocks and other furnishings with him when he went into exile in Hungary. In 1936, his belongings were auctioned off and scattered around the world. For reasons of safety and conservation, the drawings on the walls of the State Rooms are generally facsimiles.

Architekturzentrum Wien

Address: MuseumsQuartier, Museumsplatz 1
OPENING TIMES: daily 10 a.m. to 7 p.m., Wednesday until 9 p.m.
LIBRARY: Monday, Wednesday and Friday 10 a.m. to 5:30 p.m., Saturday and Sunday 10 a.m. to 7 p.m. Phone: +43/1/522 31 15
INTERNET: www.azw.at, E-MAIL: office@azw.at

The Architekturzentrum Wien (Architecture Center Vienna) encloses three sides of the Staatsratshof (State

Once Empress Sisi's pony riding hall: the library of the Architecture Center

Councilor's Courtyard) in the northern part of the MuseumsQuartier. It has a total area of approximately 1,900 m² (20,000 square feet). It consists of three halls for exhibitions and presentations, the Podium lecture hall and an open-stack library in the Oktogon, the former pony riding hall built at the request of Empress Elisabeth. It has more than 4000 titles and some 80 architecture magazines from around the world. Cafeteria Una is extremely successful from an architectural point of view: the barrel vaulting was faced with Turkish tiles by the French architects Anne Lacaton and Jean Philippe Vassal.

History: In the spring of 1992, on a commission from the City of Vienna, the architectural theorist Dietmar Steiner began to create the concept for an architecture center. A year later, in June 1993, the interim Architekturzentrum was opened in the planned MuseumsQuartier. Two halls were available, an exhibition hall (today called "the old hall") and the meeting hall, called the Podium. In the following years, the Architekturzentrum developed an active exhibition and meeting program consisting of discussions, lectures and excursions. Since 1993, it has been organizing the Viennese Architecture Congress. The year 1995 marked the founding of the architecture library, the only such resource that is publicly accessible. Also in 1995, the Architektur Archiv Austria (AAA) database was started, which has been accessible via the Internet since 1997. In the course of the MQ construction, the Architekturzentrum was enlarged to its current size. It opened on October 10, 2001.

Augustinian Church and Heart Crypt

ADDRESS: Joseph's Square. Augustinian Monastery:
Augustinerstrasse 3
MASS WITH CHOIR AND ORCHESTRA: Sunday at 11 a.m.
(except July and August)
PHONE: +43/1/533 09 47-0
INTERNET: www.augustiner.at, www.kirchenmusik-augustin.at
E-MAIL: augustinerkloster.wien@augustiner.at,
info@kirchenmusik-augustin.at

Among Vienna's medieval churches, St. Augustine's is second in size only to St. Stephen's Cathedral. It was the
Court's parish church, where Abraham a Santa Clara
preached his sermons in the 17th century. It was also the
Habsburg matrimonial church and the scene of the wedding
of Leopold I and Margaret Theresa of Spain in 1666, Maria
Theresa and Francis Stephen of Lorraine in 1736, Napoleon
(represented by Archduke Charles) and Marie-Louise in
1810, and Francis Joseph and Elisabeth in 1854.
On the wall of the right aisle is the tomb of Archduchess
Marie Christine. Commissioned by her husband, Albert,
Duke of Saxe-Teschen (founder of the ➤ **Albertina**), it was
created by Antonio Canova between 1798 and 1805. The
monument of Carrara marble depicts a funeral procession
of six figures at the entrance of a tomb, a pyramid. Among

Restored to Gothic style at the end of the 18th century: the Augustinian Church

those depicted are Virtue (with the urn of ashes) and Mercy. An oval medallion above the illusionist scenery, bordered by a serpent as the symbol of eternity and held by the floating figure of Bliss, shows the departed.

Farther to the front is a curiosity, the Heart Crypt. In 1627, the Loreto Chapel was built in the middle of the nave, in imitation of the Santa Casa. It was commissioned by Eleonora Augusta, the second wife of Ferdinand II. King Ferdinand IV (1633–1654) specified that his heart was to be buried there, and almost all the Habsburgs have followed his example. In the course of restoring the church to Gothic style in 1784, the chapel was moved to a side room. The silver urns with the hearts were placed in a double row in the crypt behind it. Every Sunday after high mass – at around 12:20 p.m. – it is possible to view the 54 urns through the barred windows in the door. Emperor Francis Joseph was the first to break this tradition by having his mortal remains, including his heart, buried next to those of Empress Elisabeth in the **Kaisergruft** (Imperial Crypt) in the Kapuzinerkirche (Church of the Capuchin Friars) (➤ **Environs**). The Gothic St. George's Chapel, which adjoins the Loreto Chapel, is a remarkable structure with two naves. It contains the tomb of Leopold II but is not open to the public.

History: In 1327, Duke Frederick I provided land southeast of the castle so the Augustinian Hermits could build a monastery. Construction of the church with three naves began three years later (the architect was Dietrich Ladtner von Pirn), and the church was consecrated in 1349. Construction of St. George's Chapel, parallel to the nave, began in 1337 on a commission from Duke Otto. The cemetery in front of the church was abandoned in 1460 and replaced by an imperial garden, which Ferdinand I used as an exercise ground. In 1634, St. Augustine formally became the parish church of the Court, and soon the interior was remodeled in the early-Baroque style with 18 side chapels. The church tower was built in 1652, and between 1767 and 1769 the façade disappeared behind the left wing of the former Court Library ➤ **Prunksaal (State Hall)**. On a commission from Emperor Joseph II in 1783, the church was restored to Gothic style by Johann Ferdinand Hetzendorf von Hohenberg and the number of monks was reduced. The last Augustinian prior died in 1837. During the fighting of the 1848 Revolution, the Court Library was set ablaze. The fire spread to the roof of the monastery and brought down the tower, which was rebuilt in 1852. The High Altar, made by Andreas Halbig between 1857 and 1870 and installed in 1874, was originally intended for the Votivkirche. After being damaged in bombing during World War II, the monastery and church were restored, and the work completed in 1950. Since 1951 the church has been back in the hands of the Augustinians. Interior restoration undertaken between 1996 and 1999 was intended to restore the church to the style of 1783.

Dschungel Wien
(Theatre for Young Audiences)

ADDRESS: MuseumsQuartier, Museumsplatz 1
PROGRAM: from early October until late May
PHONE: +43/1/522 07 20
INTERNET: www.thfk.at, E-MAIL: office@thfk.at

The 970 m² (10,400 square feet) Theatre for Young Audiences called Dschungel (Jungle), is located in the Klosterhof (Cloister Courtyard) of the MuseumsQuartier; the entrance is in the Fürstenhof (Prince's Courtyard). It has two multi-purpose halls (with seats for 100 and 180, respectively), a seminar area and a play corner. The Theatre offers guest performances as well as its own productions. In addition to conventional theatre for children and young people, it also offers marionette, puppet and dance theatre as well as music productions and plays of an experimental nature. It is also a center for providing information and continuing education in theatre for children and young people.

History: Since the early 1990s, those actively involved in staging children's theatre in Vienna had been calling for a children's playhouse of their own. Among other sites, a theatrical venue in the Spittelberg area was considered, but the project failed for lack of funds. The success of the Zoom Children's Museum led in 1997 to the idea of converting the empty premises of the former Residenz Cinema, adjoining the MuseumsQuartier on Mariahilfer Strasse, into a playhouse for children and young people. The concept and plans were presented in the summer of 2000, and in the autumn of 2002 the City of Vienna made a commitment to its realization. Construction began in the summer of 2003, and the Theatre opened on October 1, 2004.

Ephesus Museum

ADDRESS: Neue Burg, Heldenplatz (Middle Gate)
OPENING TIMES: daily except Tuesday 10 a.m. to 6 p.m.
PHONE: +43/1/525 24-476
INTERNET: www.khm.at, E-MAIL: info.as@khm.at

Ephesus, which was founded in Asia Minor by the Greeks in around 1000 BC, was one of the most important cities of classical antiquity. During its golden age (2nd century AD), some 300,000 people lived in the capital of the Roman province of Asia, where Heraclitus had once taught and where the Apostle Paul lived for two years. But it is worth visiting the Ephesus Museum not only because of the archaeological finds on display and the model of the reconstructed city (on a scale of 1:500). Not to be missed are the Neue Burg's monumental and magnificently decorated staircase, built between 1907 and 1913, in which most of the objects are exhibited, as well as the concave Marble Gallery. The admission ticket is also valid for the other collections of the ➤ **Kunsthistorisches Museum** in the Neue Burg and Corps de Logis.

Among the items on display are architectural models, reliefs, busts and small sculptures, including a bronze table candelabrum depicting the battle between Heracles and the Centaur. In addition to an

Life-size bronze statue of an athlete cleaning his strigil, or scraping iron (Roman copy)

octagonal tomb and a bronze statue of an athlete cleaning his strigil (scraping iron), the showpiece of the collection is the 40-meter (130-foot) long frieze of the
Parthian Monument, built around 170 AD to celebrate
the victory of the Roman troops over the Parthians. The
reliefs glorify the life of Emperor Lucius Aurelius Verus,
the adopted brother and son-in-law of Marcus Aurelius.
A number of finds are on display from the Temple of
Artemis, the goddess of nature and childbirth, which
was numbered among the Seven Wonders of the World,
and from the famous Library of Celsus, which was built
above the tomb of the Roman senator Tiberius Iulius
Celsus Ptolemaeanus, who died in 117 AD. Also in the
collection are architectural fragments and sculptures
connected with cult worship on the Greek island of
Samothrace. They were excavated in 1873 and 1875 by
Austrian archeologists.

History: In 1895 the Austrian Archeological Institute
began excavation work that continues today at Ephesus
(in modern Turkey). There near the village of Selçuk,
British archeologist John Turtle Wood discovered the
ruins of the Temple of Artemis in 1869. Until 1906, the
Turkish authorities granted the Austrians permission to
take numerous objects of high artistic quality to Vienna.
The finds first entered the Collection of Greek and
Roman Antiquities of the Kunsthistorisches Museum,
but because of lack of space only a small number of
them could be exhibited (sometimes in the ➤ **Temple of
Theseus** in the Volksgarten). In 1978, following four
years of planning and remodeling, the Ephesus Museum
opened in the Neue Burg as a branch of the Collection
of Greek and Roman Antiquities.

Esperanto Museum

ADDRESS: Hofburg, Michaelerkuppel
(Batthyány Staircase in Michael's Dome). From the summer of
2005: Mollard Palace, Herrengasse 9
OPENING TIMES: October to June: Monday to Wednesday 9 a.m.
to 4 p.m., Thursday noon to 7 p.m., Friday 9 a.m. to 1 p.m.
July to September: Monday to Friday 9 a.m. to 1 p.m.
PHONE: +43/1/535 51 45
(from the summer of 2005: +43/1/534 10 730)
INTERNET: www.onb.ac.at/sammlungen/plansprachen/
E-MAIL: plansprachen@onb.ac.at

The Esperanto Museum was founded in 1927 by Hugo Steiner and incorporated into the ➤ **Österreichische Nationalbibliothek (Austrian National Library)** in 1929. It has the world's largest collection of material on artificial languages, including 25,000 library volumes, 2500 periodical titles, 2000 museum objects, 2000 autographs and handwritten pieces, 20,000 photos and photo negatives, 1100 posters and 40,000 pamphlets . Esperanto is the most important of the world's 500 registered artificial languages, but the Museum documents the entire range, from Klingon (from the TV series *Star Trek*) to pan-Slavic languages developed during the period of the Austro-Hungarian Empire to the Lingua Ignota of Hildegard von Bingen.

The project Lingvo Internacia, which was presented in a thin brochure in 1887 by the Polish-Russian oculist Dr. L. L. Zamenhof writing under the pseudonym "Dr. Esperanto," has since developed into a complete language, used today by several million speakers. With the help of audiovisual media, historical documents and other objects, the Museum provides insights into the history and significance of the language. In 2005 the Esperanto Museum is moving to the recently renovated Mollard Palace, which is also the home of the ➤ **Globe Museum** and the Music Collection of the Austrian National Library.

The posters had already been printed, but the World Esperanto Congress of 1914 had to be cancelled because of the First World War

Film Museum

ADDRESS: Augustinerstrasse 1
OPENING TIMES OF THE LIBRARY:
Monday and Thursday noon to 6 p.m.
PHONE: +43/1/533 70 54
INTERNET: www.filmmuseum.at, E-MAIL: office@filmmuseum.at

The Film Museum was founded in 1964 by Peter Kon-
lechner and film artist Peter Kubelka. Its principal focus
is on the preservation, restoration, study and presentation of film as a medium. The German magazine *Der
Spiegel* called the Film Museum "one of the most agile
cinémathèques in Europe." Comprehensive retrospectives
are devoted to avant-garde film, the comedians of the
1920s and 30s, Soviet Revolutionary films, classic American film genres and Japanese cinema.

Since 1965, these retrospectives have been shown in the
Museum's own cinema. For the 25th anniversary in
1989, the "Invisible Cinema" based on a concept by
Peter Kubelka was opened: a screening room in black-
on-black design and intended as a "viewing and listening
machine" permits viewers to focus their concentration
with utmost intensity on the film being shown. Since
November 2002, the Film Museum has been equipped
with a completely renovated and extended projection
and sound system.

The Museum has a collection of more than 20,000
films. In addition to classics of international cinema
and avant-garde film, historical film documents and
newsreels, propaganda films and commercials, it contains contemporary independent cinema as well as the
works of German-speaking filmmakers in exile. The
library of the Film Museum is the largest of its kind in

Austria, with more than
16,000 books and over
200 periodicals. Use of the
library is free, but the
books cannot be checked
out. The Film Museum
currently has more than
12,000 members.

A "viewing and listening machine":
a screening room in black-on-black
design makes for "Invisible Cinema"

Pocket globe with hinged case
(England 1750)
Diameter: 7 centimeters

Globe Museum

ADDRESS: Josefsplatz 1, left side-gate.
From the summer of 2005: Mollard Palace, Herrengasse 9
OPENING TIMES: Monday to Wednesday and Friday 11 a.m.
to noon, Thursday 2 p.m. to 3 p.m.
PHONE: +43/1/534 10-297
(from the summer of 2005: +43/1/534 10-700)
INTERNET: www.onb.ac.at/sammlungen/globen/

The unique Globe Museum in the ➤ Österreichische
Nationalbibliothek (**Austrian National Library**) has a
collection of more than 400 globes and related instruments, such as armillary spheres, planetaria, lunaria and
telluria. With respect to the objects made before 1850,
the collection is the second most important in the world,
after the National Maritime Museum in Greenwich. The
oldest surviving globe in Austria (made by Rainer
Gemma Frisius about 1535) is on loan to the museum.
Around 200 exhibited objects reflect changing ideas
about cartography and cosmography as well as develop-
ments in the construction of globes down to the present
day. The museum records the history of our concept of
the shape of the earth and skies, bringing them to three-
dimensional life.

History: Globes were documented at the Imperial Court
Library from the beginning of the modern age (including an armillary sphere made by Martin Furtenbach
around 1535), but those items have been lost. The
Venetian globe-maker Vincenzo Coronelli gave Leopold
I a pair of his globes (each 110 centimeters, 43 inches in
diameter) that were lavishly colored and decorated with
a portrait of the Emperor. Together with a second,
almost identical pair of globes, they were exhibited
beneath the central dome of the State Hall in the Court
Library. A pair of globes by Gerard Mercator (1541 and

Geocentric and heliocentric armillary sphere (Vienna 1764)

1551) were acquired from a private owner in 1875. But interest in models of the earth and planets remained limited, and in 1922 there were only 14 globes in the National Library.

The Globe Museum was founded as part of the Map Department of the National Library in 1953 and opened in 1956. An important part of the holdings had been collected by the Viennese globe researcher Robert Haardt, who had established a museum in his apartment after World War II. In its first three decades, the Globe Museum's original collection of 71 items more than doubled. In 1986 it moved to new space, but as new acquisitions and loans entered the collection, the quarters soon proved to be too small. In 2005 the Museum is moving to the recently renovated Mollard Palace, which is also the home of the ➤ **Esperanto Museum** and the Music Collection of the National Library.

Halls E + G

ADDRESS: MuseumsQuartier, Museumsplatz 1
OPENING TIMES: vary depending on the event
BOX OFFICE AND ADVANCE SALES: Monday to Saturday from 10 a.m. to 7 p.m.
PHONE: +43/1/524 33 21
INTERNET: www.halleneg.at, E-MAIL: office@halleneg.at

The two performance halls, which opened in May 2001, are in and under the former Winter Riding Hall in the MuseumsQuartier. They share the entrance, box office and foyer with the ➤ **Kunsthalle Wien**, which was constructed directly behind the building. The underground Hall G is used by ➤ **Tanzquartier Wien** from September to April. In May and June both halls serve as venues for the Vienna Festival. During the remaining months, there are events of all kinds. The ingeniously illuminated foyer of Hall E is arguably the most successful architectural detail in the MuseumsQuartier.

History: The Vienna Festival is a large, comprehensive performing arts festival staged every year in early summer. Starting in 1985, various halls of the Messepalast were used as performance venues, including those called E and G. By October 1989, plans had been made to create a performance hall (in combination with the Kunsthalle), but it was not feasible to erect a dedicated building for this purpose. In the summer of 1995 it was decided to convert the Winter Riding Hall to a performance hall and to erect the Kunsthalle behind it. In 1997, a decision was made to create a second, underground hall to be used primarily for dance performances.

The Winter Riding Hall was divided into two separate spaces to improve the acoustics. Because of its length it would otherwise hardly have been suitable for spoken theatre. The separation is created by a steeply rising grandstand. Reminiscent of a ship's hull, it is set into the foyer with its central bar. The aluminum lining of the grandstand's lower surface is in contrast to the former Emperor's Box, now the home of Café-Restaurant Halle. Two free-standing staircases form a buffer between the two architectural styles: clean and contemporary on the one hand and ornamented Classicistic on the other.

Architecturally brilliant: the foyer of Hall E with the former Emperor's Box

Heldendenkmal (Heroes' Monument) and Crypt

ADDRESS: Heldenplatz
OPENING TIMES OF THE CRYPT: Tuesday to Friday
8 a.m. to 11:30 a.m. and 12:30 p.m. to 4 p.m.
MASS: every Sunday and holiday at 10 a.m.

In May 1809, a few days before the Battle of Aspern, which he was to lose, Napoleon bombarded the city of Vienna from the site of the Imperial Stables. Among the structures destroyed was the Burgtor gate. Between 1821 and 1824, in the course of converting the area to a parade ground, a new gate was built on plans by Luigi Cagnola, later modified by Pietro Nobile, to create a memorial to the Battle of the Nations at Leipzig (1813). The broad structure with five entrances separated by columns – the gateway in the middle was reserved for Court carriages – is considered the most important work of "Revolutionary Classicism" in Austria. In 1934 the Burgtor, which since 1916 had been a War Memorial (laurel wreaths with the names of fallen soldiers on the triglyph frieze), was redesigned by Rudolf Wondraček as a Heroes' Monument. Two basins for memorial flames were added on the side facing the Ring. Two monumental stairways were cut into the Burgtor on the side, leading to an open Ruhmeshalle (Hall of Glory) above the gate with its five entrances. It was dedicated to those who served in the Imperial Army from 1618 to 1918.

In the northwestern wing was the Crypt, an apsidal room flanked by columns, with the sculpture of a *Toter Krieger* (*Dead Warrior*, 1935) made by Wilhelm Frass of red marble. He also added the eagle sculptures to the gateways on either side of the Burgtor. In the Nazi daily *Völkischer Beobachter* ("People's Observer") of December 25-26, 1938, Frass, who was one of the most frequently employed

Austrian sculptors during the Nazi period, boasted that when the figure was erected, he had hidden a metal capsule with a declaration of faith in National Socialism. His wish came true on March 15, 1938,

Crypt with the sculpture of a
Dead Warrior

when Hitler laid a wreath at the feet of the statue. Despite repeated protests, the sculpture has not been removed and no one knows whether Frass's note actually exists. In the adjacent room are books with the names of Austria's fallen soldiers from both World Wars.

In 1965, the chapel for non-Catholics in the southwestern wing became a "shrine for the victims in the struggle for Austrian freedom" and since then it has also served as a mortuary. In 1991, a cast-iron cross designed by Gustav Peichl was installed on the south of the Burgtor in remembrance of the visits of Pope John Paul II to Vienna (1983 and 1998). Since 2002 there has been a metal monument north of the gate, dedicated to police officers and constables who have died in the line of duty.

Hofburg Congress Centre

ADDRESS: Heldenplatz
ADMISSION: only for public events
PHONE: +43/1/587 36 66
INTERNET: www.hofburg.com
E-MAIL: kongresszentrum@hofburg.com

The Hofburg Congress Centre is a complex of magnificent rooms that gradually grew together over the centuries. Directly connected to the ➤ Redoutensäle on Josefsplatz (Joseph's Square), it consists of 33 rooms that are used for staging events for between 60 and 3500 participants. The total area is 17,000 m² (183,000 square feet). The main entrance is in the Festival Hall Wing, which connects the Alte and the Neue Burg (Old and New Castle) with the Montoyer Wing (built between 1802 and 1806) and the Leopoldine Wing. The Festival Hall became necessary in the 20th century when the heir to the throne, Francis Ferdinand, opposed the building of an impressive throne hall as the heart of the Kaiserforum (Imperial Forum) planned by Gottfried Semper and Carl von Hasenauer. Construction of the Festival Hall Wing, which was designed by Ludwig Baumann in the style of late historicism, began in 1910. Work on the interior was halted during World War I and not completed until 1923, after the downfall of the monarchy. Since the renovation and modernization of the building in 1958, the rooms have been used primarily for holding national and international conferences. In 1969, a private company, the Vienna Congress Centre Hofburg Manage-

The Habsburg's final building project: the Festival Hall

ment Company Ltd., assumed managerial responsibility. In addition to the numerous congresses (Vienna has an outstanding reputation as a convention center), the Hofburg is also used for trade fairs (e.g. antiques), large banquets and a number of traditional Viennese balls (including those of the lawyers, doctors and hunters). The ball season opens each year with the Kaiserball (Imperial Ball) at New Year's.

Tour: On the second storey (*bel étage*) of the connecting wing are several halls, including the large Festival Hall, with three Neo-Baroque, monumental ceiling paintings executed by Alois Hans Schram between 1915 and 1918, octagonal paintings by Viktor Stauffer in the vaulting and lunettes by Eduard Veith. The decoration is an allegory of the House of Habsburg as the savior of the Christian West under the patronage of *Magna*

Mater Austriae and as the patron of art and science.
The Ceremonial Hall on the northwest is reached by crossing the Side Gallery. The hall was designed by Louis Montoyer and has 24 Corinthian columns of yellow faux marble and a coffered ceiling in the Classicist style. The 26 double crystal chandeliers formerly lit the room with 1300 wax candles. The hall was used as a throne room until 1918 as well as for concerts, wedding banquets and various balls. Here the Emperor conferred honors on noblemen, and the imperial couple conducted an annual foot-washing ceremony on Maundy Thursday. In this hall, Napoleon also courted Archduchess Marie-Louise, whom he married in 1810.
The Marble Hall on the northwest, which in imitation of the Ceremonial Hall was clad in faux marble in 1841, is in the Leopoldine Wing. It adjoins the Secret Privy Chamber with its original Rococo stucco ceiling. This is where Emperor Francis Joseph gave speeches to open the meetings of the Austro-Hungarian delegation. The other rooms of the Leopoldine Wing, which were the apartments of Empress Maria Theresa and Joseph II, have housed the President's Offices since 1946. The entrance to the ➤ **Präsidentschaftskanzlei (Presidential Offices)** is on Ballhausplatz.
On the southeast is the Trabantenstube (Chamber of the Guards, where the bodyguards kept watch) and the Rittersaal (Knights' Hall). These two rooms are in the oldest part of the complex, in the former "palas" of the late-medieval fortress, and together were once the Tanzhaus (Dance House). Starting in 1657, they were used by Leopold I for official functions, a purpose that continued after 1666 when the Leopoldine Wing was finished. Maria Theresa was christened in the Rittersaal in 1717. The baptismal font was set with precious stones and contained holy water to which five drops from the River Jordan had been added. In the course of general renovation in 1749, the room was redecorated in Rococo style.
The Rittersaal is adjoined by the Radetzky Apartments, where Field Marshal Johann Joseph Wenzel Count Radetzky, a personal friend of Emperor Francis Joseph I, lived after the revolutionary events of 1848. The Belgian tapestries are from the 16th and 17th centuries. Before the Neue Burg was built, the Botschafterstiege (Ambassador's Staircase) in the Schweizerhof (Swiss Court) provided access to the State Rooms. The staircase was built between 1749 and 1751 by Jean-Nicolas Jadot.

Hofburg Chapel

ADDRESS: Hofburg, Schweizerhof
OPEN TO VISITORS: from September to June, Monday to
Thursday 11 a.m. to 3 p.m., Friday 11 a.m. to 1 p.m.,
Sunday 8:15 a.m. to 10:45 a.m.
OPENING TIMES OF THE BOX OFFICE: Friday 11 a.m. to 1 p.m.
and 3 p.m. to 5 p.m., Sunday 8:15 a.m. to 9:15 a.m.
PHONE: +43/1/533 99 27
E-MAIL: hmk@aon.at, INTERNET: www.bmbwk.gv.at/hmk

The Hofburg Chapel, restored in 1977, is the home of the
Hofmusikkapelle (Court Orchestra and Choir) and thus also
of the Vienna Boys' Choir. Their musical performances can
be heard every Sunday at 9:15 a.m. from mid-September to
June (standing room is free), when the Hofmusikkapelle –
members of the Vienna Philharmonic, the men of the State
Opera Choir and the Vienna Boys' Choir – performs a mass.
On the tabernacle of the main altar is a wooden crucifix
with a legend: pursued by Protestants, the counter-
reformer Ferdinand II sought refuge beneath the black-
painted cross on June 19, 1619. It is said to have com-
forted him with the words "Ferdinand, I will not forsake
you." And in fact, Ferdinand was rescued from this difficult situation by the arrival of the Dampierre regiment.

History: Founded by Albert I, the Hofburg Chapel was first
mentioned in 1296. In 1424, the Gothic choir was added,
and interior improvements were made in the second quarter of the 15th century. The chapel was dedicated in 1449 to
the "Most Holy Trinity and All the Saints." On July 7,
1498, Maximilian I reorganized the Hofburg Chapel under
the direction of Bishop Slatkonia, a date that is considered
to mark the founding of the Hofmusikkapelle and the Hofsängerknaben (Court Orchestra and Boys' Choir). During
the Baroque period, music was accorded great importance:
Ferdinand III, Leopold I and Joseph I were composers
themselves, and under Charles VI, Johann Joseph Fux was
Hofkapellmeister (Court Composer and Music Director).
During the reign of Maria Theresa the orchestra's importance declined, its function being restricted to liturgical
services and entertaining the imperial household. In 1748
the Empress replaced the wooden altars with marble ones,
"Ferdinand's Cross" was mounted on the tabernacle, and
three new galleries as well as 12 oratories were added. The
richly decorated façade of the chapel was lost when the
Botschafterstiege (Ambassador's Staircase) was built

between 1749 and 1751. The renovations ordered by Francis II/I led to the restoration of the chapel to "Gothic" style as it was understood during the Romantic period: tracery was added to the galleries and oratories and a new pulpit in Gothic style was made. Almost nothing remains of the previous decoration, with the exception of 13 wooden statues (ca. 1480) that decorated the pillars. From 1788 to 1824 Antonio Salieri was Hofkapellmeister, but the Hofburg Chapel soon lost its significance once again: the Gesellschaft der Musikfreunde (Society of Friends of Music – the Musikverein) was founded in 1812 and became the focus of musical life. Even after the downfall of the monarchy, the Hofmusikkapelle continued to perform, responsibility for it having been transferred to the Education Ministry. The Institut der Hofsängerknaben (Boys' Choir Institute) was closed in 1920 but was reestablished in 1924 on a private basis. The name Wiener Sängerknaben (Vienna Boys' Choir) did not become established until 1928.

Hofjagd- und Rüstkammer (Collection of Arms and Armour)

ADDRESS: Neue Burg (Central Gate), Heldenplatz
OPENING TIMES: daily except Tuesday 10 a.m. to 6 p.m.
PHONE: +43/1/525 24-462
INTERNET: www.khm.at, E-MAIL: info.hjrk@khm.at

Unique: the "Eagle Armour" made by Jörg Seusenhofer (1547)

The Collection of Arms and Armour of the ➤ **Kunsthistorisches Museum** on the third floor of the Corps de Logis and in the Marble Gallery of the Neue Burg is the most important and best-documented collection of its kind in the Western world. There are objects representing almost every European monarch and prince from the 15th to the early 20th century, and the helmets and suits of armour on display were custom-made by the most renowned armourers. There are also decoratively etched swords, shields and daggers as well as beautifully ornamented rifles, pistols and shotguns from the 16th to the 19th century. Some of the suits of armour on display were intended for use in battle, but most of them – like the weapons – either resulted from the need for ostentation or were used for sport at court.

History: The armoury can be traced back to Emperor Frederick III (1425–1463). While the weapons were originally stored in the castle itself and in the abandoned Church of St. Paul, they were moved to the Stallburg at the end of the 16th century. The focus at that time was the collection of arms and armour of Emperor Maximilian II (1527–1576) and of his brothers, Ferdinand and Charles. Most of the objects – including the most beautiful ones – once belonged to them.

In 1606 Emperor Rudolf II acquired the collections at Ambras Castle near Innsbruck in Tirol. They had been accumulated by Ferdinand II (1529–1595) and included his extraordinary Heldenrüstkammer (the Atrium Hero-

NOEL COWARD THEATRE

DELFONT MACKINTOSH THEATRES

St Martin's Lane, WC2N 4AU
0844 482 5141

HAY FEVER

7:30 PM

Wednesday 16-May-2012

STALLS
E17

Ms Mike Harreld

Standard
Booking ref:
5190896
£52.50 + 1.00
Restoration Levy
+ 1.75 Bkg Fee

PLEASE CHECK YOUR TICKETS CAREFULLY AS MISTAKES CANNOT BE RECTIFIED AT A LATER DATE
TICKETS ARE SOLD SUBJECT TO THE TERMS AND CONDITIONS OVERLEAF

Terms & Conditions

1. Tickets are sold subject to the Producer's right to make any alterations to the advertised time, programme or cast as a result of circumstances beyond their control.

2. If a performance is cancelled ticket holders will first be offered alternative performances (subject to availability) up to the seat value on the ticket.

3. Tickets cannot be refunded, but they may be exchanged up to 24 hours prior to performance, subject to a per ticket fee.

4. Every member of the audience, including children, must be in possession of a valid ticket, which must be produced to gain entry to the theatre.

5. If tickets are resold or transferred for profit or commercial gain by anyone other than the Venue Management, Producer or one of their authorised agents, then they will become void and the holder may be refused entry or ejected from the venue.

6. Latecomers will be admitted to the auditorium when a suitable break in the performance occurs but admission cannot always be guaranteed.

7. Age restrictions for children may apply due to the nature and suitability of the show.

8. The Theatre Management reserves the right to refuse admission in reasonable circumstances, or eject patrons behaving in a violent or obnoxious manner.

9. The ticket holder only has a right to a seat to the value corresponding to that stated on the ticket and the management reserves the right to provide alternative seats.

10. Any comments or complaints should be made promptly to the Theatre Manager before or during the performance, or in writing to: Operations Director, Delfont Mackintosh Theatres Ltd, Novello Theatre, Aldwych, London WC2B 4LD

Full terms and conditions are available at the theatre box office or online

www.delfontmackintosh.co.uk

Like us on Facebook

facebook.com/DelfontMackintoshTheatres

twitter.com/DMTWestend

NOEL COWARD THEATRE

St Martin's Lane, WC2N 4AU
0844 482 5141

DELFONT
MACKINTOSH
THEATRES

HAY FEVER

7:30 PM

Wednesday 16-May-2012

STALLS
E18

Ms Mike Harreld

Standard
Booking ref:
5190896
£52.50 + 1.00
Restoration Levy
+ 1.75 Bkg Fee

PLEASE CHECK YOUR TICKETS CAREFULLY AS MISTAKES CANNOT BE RECTIFIED AT A LATER DATE
TICKETS ARE SOLD SUBJECT TO THE TERMS AND CONDITIONS OVERLEAF

Terms & Conditions

1. Tickets are sold subject to the Producer's right to make any alterations to the advertised time, programme or cast as a result of circumstances beyond their control.

2. If a performance is cancelled ticket holders will first be offered alternative performances (subject to availability) up to the seat value on the ticket.

3. Tickets cannot be refunded, but they may be exchanged up to 24 hours prior to a performance, subject to a per ticket fee.

4. Every member of the audience, including children, must be in possession of a valid ticket, which must be produced to gain entry to the theatre.

5. If tickets are resold or transferred for profit or commercial gain by anyone other than the Venue Management, Producer or one of their authorised agents, then they will become void and the holder may be refused entry or ejected from the venue.

6. Latecomers will be admitted to the auditorium when a suitable break in the performance occurs but admission cannot always be guaranteed.

7. Age restrictions for children may apply due to the nature and suitability of the show.

8. The Theatre Management reserves the right to refuse admission in reasonable circumstances, or eject patrons behaving in a violent or obnoxious manner.

9. The ticket holder only has a right to a seat corresponding to that stated on the ticket and the management reserves the right to provide alternative seats.

10. Any comments or complaints should be made promptly to the Theatre Manager before or during the performance, or in writing to: Operations Director, Delfont Mackintosh Theatres Ltd, Novello Theatre, Aldwych, London WC2B 4LD

Full terms and conditions are available at the theatre box office or online

www.delfontmackintosh.co.uk

Like us on Facebook

facebook.com/DelfontMackintoshTheatres

twitter.com/DMTWestEnd

icum – Armoury of Heroes). For the next two centuries they remained in Tirol. The armoury in the Stallburg continued to grow steadily as each new ruler added his splendid personal weapons and trophies (e. g. from the victorious battles against the Turks). In 1750, Empress Maria Theresa moved all of it to the armoury on Renngasse, putting it on display in a Baroque pantheon of Austrian and Habsburg history. On the orders of Joseph II, the armoury of Archduke Charles, which was stored in Graz, was added to the Vienna collection in 1765.

In 1859, the Renngasse armoury was torn down and the collection was moved to the newly constructed Arsenal, where it was combined with ostentatious weapons from Laxenburg Palace and the most beautiful items in the Hofjagd- und Sattelkammer (Collection of Arms, Armour and Saddles) to create the "k. u. k. Hof-Waffensammlung" (Imperial and Royal Court Arms Collection). Together with the Ambras collection, which had been moved to Vienna in 1806 and was on display at the Lower Belvedere Palace after 1814, these holdings were moved in 1888 to the Kunsthistorisches Museum, which opened three years later. After the downfall of the monarchy, the inventory continued to grow with additions from other court collections. Because there was no room for such a large collection, all of it was moved into the Neue Burg in 1935. The collection was removed and hidden during World War II and did not reopen until 1973.

Imperial magnificence and elegant materials: the Marble Gallery in the Neue Burg

Kaiserappartements (Imperial Apartments) and Sisi Museum

ADDRESS: Michael's Wing (entrance beneath the dome)
OPENING TIMES: daily 9 a.m. to 5 p.m. (in July and August
9 a.m. to 5:30 p.m.)
GUIDED TOURS (in German): daily at 10 a.m., 11:30 a.m. and 2 p.m.
PHONE: +43/1/533 75 70
E-MAIL: info@hofburg-wien.at, INTERNET: www.hofburg-wien.at

Visiting the apartments of Emperor Francis Joseph and
Empress Elisabeth (the ticket is also valid for admission to
the ➤ **Silver Collection**) is a highly recommended way to
begin exploring the Hofburg. The tour begins with information about the Habsburg dynasty and the architectural
history of the Hofburg. A model on a scale of 1:200,
which was made at the beginning of the 20th century, still
shows the Hofspital (Court Hospital) and the Ballhaus
(Real Tennis Courts, torn down in 1903) as well as the
downsized 1907 variant of the Kaiserforum (Imperial
Forum), with a sweeping colonnade instead of a second
wing. Like the earlier, more grandiose plans, this was
never realized either.

Tour: The entrance to the apartments is via the Kaiser-
stiege (Imperial Staircase) in the Imperial Chancellery
Wing, the same stairs that Francis Joseph used to gain

access to his apartments. In the first six rooms (Stephen's Apartment), the Sisi Museum was installed in 2004, not only maintaining the legend of the beautiful Empress but also offering a more critical view of her life. The focus of this theatrical production, which begins with her assassination in Geneva in 1898, is the private side of Elisabeth: rebelling against life at court, seeking refuge in the cult of her own beauty, dieting obsessively and writing effusive poetry.

Some 200 objects are on display. In addition to lots of memorabilia (medals, coins, commemorative pictures, small busts, etc.) and the well-known portraits, they also include the assassin's weapon – a triangular file with a wooden handle – and the death mask made by Franz von Matsch around 1900. The main focus is on the personal possessions of the Empress: we see her marriage contract, diamond stars and other jewelry, a dressing gown, fans, gloves and parasols, sets of writing utensils, a menu and scales, a black lace shawl, her death certificate and her last will and testament.

The tour takes us through 18 rooms, which either have their original furnishings or have been reconstructed from photographs. The imperial couple moved here after their wedding in 1854. The rooms were furnished according to the tastes of the time (furniture in the style of Neo-Rococo and walls clad in red silk damask). We reach the Audience Chamber via the Trabantenstube (Guard-room), where the body guards kept watch, and the Wartesaal (Waiting Room). Francis Joseph gave two general audiences a week, and every subject of the realm had the right to attend. Those attending an audience were required to appear in uniform, tail-coat or national costume. As a rule the Emperor received them at his standing desk. The Conference Room was used by the ministers for their meetings, which were

Emperor Francis Joseph always had eyes for Elisabeth: His Majesty's Study

Empress Elisabeth

Elisabeth Amalie Eugenie von Wittelsbach, called Sisi, was born in Munich on December 24, 1837. In the summer of 1853 she happened to accompany her mother and elder sister Helene to Ischl to celebrate the birthday of her cousin, Emperor Francis Joseph. Although Helene was intended to become the Emperor's bride, he fell head over heels in love with the shy Sisi and immediately became engaged. On April 24, 1854, they were married in the Church of the Augustinian Friars in Vienna. In 1855 their daughter Sophie was born (she died in 1857), in 1856 Gisela, and in 1858 Crown Prince Rudolf.

Elisabeth fulfilled her duties as Empress with reluctance. On official occasions she felt as though she were being paraded like a horse "in harness." In addition, her marriage with the pedantic and conservative Francis Joseph entered a crisis that reached its height in 1860. In 1866, Elisabeth spoke out in favor of greater autonomy for Hungary, and a year later the Dual Monarchy of Austria-Hungary was established. Francis Joseph and Elisabeth were crowned king and queen of Hungary. Elisabeth's favorite daughter, Marie Valerie, was born in 1868.

called "*Minister Conseils*." The Emperor, who usually arose at 3:30 a.m., spent most of his waking hours in his Study. Across from his writing-desk is his favorite portrait of the Empress. It was in this room on January 30, 1889, that he received the news of the suicide of his only son, Rudolf. The simple furnishings of the bedroom are evidence that Francis Joseph rejected luxury of every kind. He was perfectly happy with a simple dressing table and an iron bed.

When he wanted to visit the Empress, whose rooms were around the corner in the Amalia Wing, he had to ring a bell hidden behind a curtain in the Smoking Room (today a memorial room to Emperor Maximilian of Mexico) and ask to be admitted. This apartment with its large living room and bedroom was decorated in Neo-Rococo style,

Sisi suffered increasingly from the loss of her personal freedom and wrote poetry: "I have awakened in a dungeon/ With chains on my hands/And my longing ever stronger/ And Freedom! You, turned from me!" She reacted to the constraints of the Vienna Court by taking refuge in her own beauty, obsessive dieting and sporting manias (riding, fencing, swimming). She spent increasing time in travel. Although she was embarrassed by her dark teeth, Elisabeth allowed her portrait to be painted one last time in 1879 at the age of 42.

Elisabeth became even more withdrawn and eccentric after the suicide of her only son, Rudolf, in 1889, after he had shot and killed his mistress, Mary Vetsera, at Mayerling Hunting Lodge. Sisi's request to travel to America was denied. She gave away her jewelry and took to wearing only black. She even gave up writing poetry. On September 10, 1898, the Empress, who was traveling under the name Countess of Hohenembs, was assassinated in Geneva by the Italian anarchist Luigi Lucheni.

Her immortality began with her tragic death, and a legend grew up in keeping with the one fostered by the Empress's unconventional lifestyle. The memory today of the good, beautiful and selfless Empress has been strengthened by numerous films (including Ernest Marischka's *Sisi* series with Romy Schneider). But as we know from contemporary newspaper accounts, Elisabeth was neither particularly admired nor popular during her lifetime.

Here the "Minister Conseils" were held: the Conference Room

Wall-bars and rings: Elisabeth's dressing and exercise room

but some of the stucco decorations date from the 18th century. The wall-bars and rings that Elisabeth mounted in her dressing room and the doorway to the Large Salon create a rather strange impression. They were used for her daily program of exercises. In 1876, Elisabeth became the first member of the imperial family to have her own bathroom, with a bathtub of galvanized copper. Behind the bathroom are the two Bergl Rooms, which are covered in exotic landscape murals painted in 1766 by Johann Bergl. The original purpose of these rooms is not clear. In Elisabeth's day they were probably used by court servants as dressing rooms and lounges.

The Empress gained access to her apartments by climbing the Adlerstiege (Eagle's Staircase) in the adjoining Leopoldine Wing and by passing through the Türhüterzimmer (Doorkeeper's Room). The Large Antechamber that adjoins the Small Salon was a meeting place for the imperial family when they were going to a court ball. Led by the Master of Ceremonies, they crossed the State Rooms in the Leopoldine Wing (apartment of Maria Theresa, today the ➤ **Präsidentschaftskanzlei (Presidential Offices)** to the Ceremonial Hall.

Alexander's Apartments adjoined the Large Antechamber on the northwest. Here Tsar Alexander of Russia resided during the Congress of Vienna, and the last Austrian emperor, Charles I, lived here from 1916 to 1918. The Red Salon is decorated with Gobelin tapestries made in Paris; the medallions were modeled on paintings by François Boucher. The tapestries were a gift from Louis XVI to his brother-in-law Emperor Joseph II.

In Emperor Franz Joseph's day, the Dining Room was used mostly for family dinners, which followed strict court ceremonial, the Emperor sitting at mid-table. A dinner consisted of between nine and 13 courses and never lasted more than 45 minutes. The White Hall and an antechamber take us to the Alexanderstiege (Alexander's Staircase) on Schauflergasse, and we leave the Amalia Wing. The other rooms surrounding the courtyard were the private apartment of Emperor Charles. Today they are government offices.

Kunsthalle Wien

ADDRESS: MuseumsQuartier, Museumsplatz 1
OPENING TIMES: Friday to Tuesday 10 a.m. to 7 p.m.,
Thursday to 10 p.m.
PHONE: +43/1/521 89-33
INTERNET: www.kunsthallewien.at
E-MAIL: office@kunsthallewien.at

Kunsthalle Wien in the MuseumsQuartier is an urban exhibition space for international contemporary art. In the year 2002 the Italian art magazine *Arte* listed it on a footing with the Centre Pompidou in Paris and the Tate Modern in London as one of the six best institutions for exhibitions in Europe. The program focuses on photography, video, film, installations and new media. The Kunsthalle is a functional building, whose red brick emphasizes the workshop character of the art center. It is accessed through a converted gateway attached to the right side of the Winter Riding Hall. A shared entrance hall provides access to the Exhibition Hall and the Performance Halls (➤ **Halls E + G**). Hall 2, on the ground floor, serves primarily for presenta-

Vaulted ceiling: Hall I on the upper floor of Kunsthalle Wien

tions of contemporary expositions and retrospectives of young artists. Hall 1, on the upper floor, extends across the entire length (57 meters, 181 feet) of the building wing. Its hallmark is a vaulted ceiling that is more reminiscent of a cathedral than of an "art factory." Hall 1 is used primarily for large thematic exhibitions as well as for displaying important individual positions. The levels are connected by two prominent, free-standing staircases. The entrance hall provides access to the façade of the Kunsthalle. The band of illuminated display cases serves as a "project wall" in the public area.

History: The City of Vienna had been organizing exhibitions in the Messepalast since 1988 and planned to establish an arts center there. Because the MuseumsQuartier was not expected to open before 1994-95, an interim solution was found, a temporary arts center on Karlsplatz. When the yellow and blue painted container designed by Alfred Krischanitz opened in September 1992, many Viennese considered it to be an ugly box. Starting in December 1995, in order to create an immediate presence on the future cultural site, performances were continually staged in a hall of the Messepalast. The new Kunsthalle finally opened in February 2001 with a performance by Vanessa Beecroft. Regular programming began in May 2001. But the Karlsplatz location was not entirely abandoned. The "box" was replaced by a glass pavilion, also a very successful design by Krischanitz. Since January 2002 it has been serving as exhibition space for projects focused on specific topics.

Kunsthistorisches Museum

ADDRESS: Maria-Theresien-Platz
OPENING TIMES: daily except Monday 10 a.m. to 6 p.m.,
Picture Gallery and Egyptian and Near Eastern Collection,
Thursday 10 a.m. to 9 p.m.
GUIDED TOURS ON SPECIAL TOPICS: every Wednesday and Friday
10:15 a.m.; every Tuesday and Thursday 12:30 p.m. ("Mittags
im KHM"); every Thursday 6:30 p.m. ("Alte Meister")
PHONE: +43/1/525 24-0
INTERNET: www.khm.at, E-mail: info@khm.at

In Thomas Bernhard's novel *Alte Meister* ("Old Masters"),
the music philosopher Reger is heard to grumble at length
about the Kunsthistorisches Museum and the Habsburgs,
to whom the Museum owes its enormous collections,
because the Museum "doesn't even have a Goya, not even
an El Greco." The Museum gets along just fine without
an El Greco, who is not considered to have been among
the top echelon of painters, but not to have a Goya is
"downright fatal" for a museum like the Kunsthistorisches. Things are, of course, not as bad as Bernhard, a
master of exaggeration, would have one believe. The
KHM has a wonderful Vermeer ("Allegory of Painting"),
the world's largest collection of works by Pieter Bruegel
the Elder as well as countless other masterpieces, including works by Jan van Eyck, Hieronymus Bosch, Albrecht
Dürer, Titian, Tintoretto, Veronese, Parmigianino,
Giuseppe Arcimboldo,
Peter Paul Rubens and
Diego Rodríguez de Silva
y Velázquez.
In addition, the Kunsthistorisches Museum, which
was dedicated by Emperor
Francis Joseph to "the
monuments of art and
antiquity," consists of far
more than just its Picture
Gallery. It also has the Collection of Sculpture and
Decorative Arts, Collection
of Greek and Roman
Antiquities, Egyptian and
Near Eastern Collection
and a Coin Cabinet that

Jan Vermeer:
"Allegory of Painting" (1665/1666)

with 700,000 objects (coins, paper money, medals and decorations) is one of the most important in the world. Because of lack of space in the main building, the ➤ Hofjagd- und Rüstkammer (Collection of Arms and Armour) as well as the ➤ Sammlung alter Musikinstrumente (Collection of Ancient Musical Instruments) had to be moved. Together with the ➤ Ephesus Museum (part of the Collection of Greek and Roman Antiquities) and the ➤ Museum

Cupola Hall and Staircase: "Theseus and the Centaur" by Antonio Canova

of Ethnology they are across the street, in the Neue Burg and the Corps de Logis.

History: For centuries the imperial collections were scattered across various parts of the Hofburg and the Belvedere Palace, where the Picture Gallery was opened to the public in 1781. Plans to construct new buildings to house the collections date from the early 19th century. But the project did not become concrete until the city wall was demolished on the orders of Emperor Francis Joseph (1857) and the new Ringstrasse was laid out. In 1862 the architect Ludwig Förster proposed building two Court

Museums on the former glacis between the Hofburg and the Imperial Stables: the Kunsthistorisches and the ➤ **Naturhistorisches Museum**. In 1864 Francis Joseph gave his approval, and in 1866 four architects – Heinrich von Ferstel, Theophil von Hansen, Moritz Ritter von Löhr and Carl von Hasenauer – were invited to submit plans for two buildings that were to be mirror images of each other.

The jury, however, came to the conclusion that none of the four submitted designs was suitable. Thus they invited the German architect Gottfried Semper to come to Vienna to evaluate the plans. He criticized not only the plans themselves but also the competition's frame of reference and called for a comprehensive new concept that was to include the idea of a Kaiserforum (Imperial Forum). The Emperor commissioned him to develop a concept based on one of the existing plans. Semper chose Hasenauer's design, but made some fundamental changes that caused great tension between the two architects. In 1870 Francis Joseph approved the plan for the Kaiserforum, and ground was broken in the autumn of 1871. In 1880 the two buildings were finished, but the magnificent interior design, which Hasenauer undertook alone, was not yet complete. The Naturhistorisches Museum opened in 1889; the Kunsthistorisches Museum followed two years later.

All four façades of the Kunsthistorisches Museum are decorated with numerous figures. They depict allegories as well as historical personages and artists. The iconological program was designed by Semper and illustrates the conditions governing the creation of a work of art: material aspects dominate the ground floor, artistic ones the main floor, and both are surmounted on the attic floor and along the balustrade by the individual as the crowning glory, the statues depicting famous artists. The program is in chronological order, leading from classical antiquity (Babenbergerstrasse) to the Middle Ages (the side facing the MuseumsQuartier) to the Renaissance (Maria Theresa Square) to the Modern Age (Ring). The lantern in the cupola is crowned with a statue by Johann Benk of Pallas Athena as the protectress of the arts and sciences.

Tour: The view from the Entrance Hall through the circular opening in the Cupola Hall above it is breathtaking.

Before we climb the Main Staircase to the Picture Gallery, we turn right and enter the Egyptian and Near Eastern Collection on the mezzanine floor. The first two large Rooms (I and V) demonstrate the idea of an historical *Gesamtkunstwerk* ("total work of art") in an impressive manner. The painted ceilings are supported by three original papyrus columns of granite; the walls are decorated with scenic pictures and hieroglyphic inscriptions. Even the doorways are in Egyptian style.

The parts of the collection on display are organized into various subdivisions: the focus is on the Egyptian cult of the dead and religion as well as on the plastic arts, especially sculpture. The museum's rich holdings are based on a major acquisition in 1821 as well as the Miramar Collection of Archduke Ferdinand Max (who as Emperor Maximilian of Mexico was executed there in 1867). The important collection of monuments from the Old Kingdom is the result of Austrian excavations between 1912 and 1929 in the cemetery of Giza. Extremely interesting are the Tomb Chapel of Ka-ninisut and the False Door of Iha, which were found in the cemetery to the west of the Cheops Pyramid in Giza. In a small display case you'll find the mascot of the Kunsthistorisches Museum, a 20-centimeter (8-inch) long hippopotamus of blue faience (placed in a tomb around 2000 BC). Painted on the hippo's body are signs of its habitat (papyrus, lotus, a bird) to indicate that it is wallowing in a swampy landscape.

The Collection of Greek and Roman Antiquities is displayed in adjoining rooms to the south. The holdings range from Cypriot Bronze Age pottery from the 3rd millennium BC to Slavic finds from around 1000 AD. The architecture of Room XI is copied from the Roman imperial age. The imitative relief frieze with the legends of the gods is by August Eisenmenger. The collection, which will reopen in the autumn of 2004 after four years of renovation, is internationally renowned for its spectacular gems and cameos (Ptolemaic Cameo, Eagle Cameo, Gemma Augustea) as well as its finds from the time of the Great Migration (Tomb of the Princess of Untersiebenbrunn) and the

Middle Ages (Hoard of Gold from Nagyszentmiklós).
Among the newly exhibited items are reliefs from the
Heroon of Trysa, a tomb in ancient Lycia (today in
southwestern Turkey), which is one of the most important objects in the collection of ancient sculpture. One
gallery explains the development of the Roman portrait
from the 1st century BC to painted mummy portraits.
The smaller rooms have a thematic focus (Cyprus,
Etruria, lower Italy as well as Austria Romana). The
larger-than-life bronze statue of the *Youth from the
Magdalensberg* has proved a disappointment in one
respect: until the 1980s it was considered to be an original from the 1st century AD. But it is "only" a copy
made after a farmer found the original while plowing in
1502. The genuine statue disappeared and was taken to
Spain under mysterious circumstances.

The eastern wing, which originally housed the Münz-
kabinett (Coin Cabinet, now in three specially adapted
and spacious rooms on the third floor) and the Collections of Arms and Armour and of Ancient Musical
Instruments, is now home to the Collection of Sculpture and Decorative Arts, which includes some 800
tapestries. The high quality of the collection resulted
from combining the Kunst- und Wunderkammer (arts
and natural wonders rooms) of Archduke Ferdinand II
at Ambras Castle near Innsbruck and of Emperor
Rudolf II from Prague Castle as well as the collection

Gesamtkunstwerk: the rooms of the Egyptian and Near Eastern Collection

Impressive stairwell: lunettes by Hans Makart

of Archduke Leopold William and former holdings of
the ➤ **Schatzkammer (Treasury)** in the Hofburg.
The collection has an astonishing variety of objects: in
addition to sculptures of every conceivable material, it
has vessels of precious stones, ivory carvings and gold-
smith work as well as games, cabinets, toilet and other
caskets, clocks, automatons and other complicated
instruments. It is still not clear what the "Püsterich"
(Fire-Blower), a 25-centimeter (10-inch) bronze figure
from the 12th century, was used for. The little man, who
is reproduced on many KHM products, was filled with
water and placed among the embers, where he puffed
steam through small holes in his mouth and nose. The
most famous item in the collection, the "Saliera" by
Benvenuto Cellini (an ornate saltcellar of gold and
enamel) was stolen in May 2003. The Collection of
Sculpture and Decorative Arts, which has been closed
for renovation since 2002, is to reopen in 2005.
A staircase of white Carrara marble leads to the second
floor. On the landing stands the sculpture "Theseus
and the Centaur" by Antonio Canova. Created between
1805 and 1819, it was originally intended as a symbol
of Napoleon; the symbolism was reinterpreted after his
defeat. For this sculpture, made on a commission from
Emperor Francis II/I, Pietro Nobile built the ➤ **Temple**

of **Theseus** in the Volksgarten between 1819 and 1823. In 1890 the piece was moved to this central location in the Kunsthistorisches Museum to complete the interior furnishings.

The large ceiling fresco in the stairway is entitled "Apotheosis of the Renaissance" and was painted by the Hungarian artist Mihály von Munkácsy. The viewer steps into the painting like the man on the lower edge of the picture. The fanlights in the staircase present Renaissance masters, including Michelangelo, Veronese, Titian, Leonardo da Vinci and Raphael. Each of the four sides has three lunettes by Hans Makart. The spandrel pictures between the capitals of the huge columns are by Gustav Klimt, Ernest Klimt and Franz von Matsch. They depict the development of art (a sign near the Cupola Hall explains the individual pictures in detail). Gustav Klimt, who with his brother and Matsch also painted the ceiling frescoes above the Main Staircase of the **Burgtheater** (➤ Environs), was responsible here for "Egypt" and "Greek Classicism."

The Picture Gallery spreads across the entire second floor. Italian, Spanish and French pictures are found in the southwestern wing; the northeastern wing has Dutch, Flemish and German paintings. The foundations for the Picture Gallery were laid by Archduke Leopold William during his governorship in the Netherlands from 1647 to 1656. He acquired some 1400 pictures, mostly Renaissance Venetian painting (Titian, Veronese, Tintoretto) as well as major works by Flemish masters of the 15th to the 17th century (van Eyck, Rubens, van Dyck). In 1651 David Teniers the Younger painted the Archduke with several visitors at his picture gallery in Brussels, and the 51 Italian paintings that are depicted are

Klimt painting: "Egypt"

Raphael: "Madonna in the Meadow" (1505 or 1506)

mostly in the Kunsthistorisches Museum today. The KHM's gallery portrait was one of a series that Leopold William commissioned to document his collection.

In addition, the Archduke tried to acquire paintings for the collection of his brother Emperor Ferdinand III at Prague Castle after it was looted by the Swedes. The collection had been founded decades earlier by Emperor Rudolf II (1552–1612), a great lover of art. In the early 18th century, Charles VI decided to bring together the Habsburg's painting collections in Vienna. Leopold William's collection was put on display in the Baroque manner in the Stallburg along with holdings from Prague Castle and several other palaces. In 1728 in the course of this rearrangement, Charles VI commissioned the Neapolitan painter Francesco Solimena to create a large painting that would be a monument to the Emperor and his artistic sensibilities: with a solemn gesture the Imperial Minister of Buildings, Gundacker Ludwig Joseph Count Althan, hands the Emperor a three-volume inventory of the Imperial Picture Gallery. This painting can be seen in Room VII, and if it seems a bit odd, that is because the court painter Johann Gottfried Auerbach added the faces of Charles VI and Althan to the otherwise finished painting.

In 1776, Empress Maria Theresa decided to open the Picture Gallery in the Upper Belvedere Palace to the public. By 1781, the paintings had been put on display in accordance with historical criteria. Under her son Joseph II, the collection grew rapidly as Flemish and Italian paintings were added, most of them large-format altar paintings taken from the monasteries and churches that had been dissolved. Many artworks were lost when Napoleon conquered Vienna in 1809, and during the next century almost nothing was added to the collection.

There are many paintings here that simply should not be missed: the Vermeer and Rembrandt's self-portraits, the "Madonna in the Meadow" by Raphael, the "Self-portrait in a Convex Mirror" by Parmigianino and "Christ Carrying the Cross" by Hieronymus Bosch. It is worth taking extra time to study the unbelievably detailed paintings by Pieter Bruegel the Elder, including "The Fight Between Carnival and Lent," "Children's Games" and "The Tower of Babel." Viewing the "Peasant Wedding" you may legitimately wonder why the red-jacketed man carrying the pies has three legs. Another strange detail is the superfluous river in "The Assumption of the Virgin Mary" by Peter Paul Rubens. According to the music philosopher Reger in Thomas Bernhard's novel *Old Masters*, if you study a painting long enough, you will eventually discover a serious mistake.

Or you can simply enjoy the fantastic details: for example, the wonderfully evil cat in "The Feast of the Bean King" by Jacob Jordaens or the mouth of the dragon at the feet of "Saint Margaret" by Raphael and his studio. And the allegorical depictions of the seasons and elements by Giuseppe Arcimboldo are always popular. He was court painter from 1562 to 1587 under the emperors Ferdinand I, Maximilian II and Rudolf II. The 13 views of Vienna and imperial palaces painted by Bernardo Bellotto (Canaletto) between 1758 and 1761 on a commission from Empress Maria Theresa give us a highly interesting impression of the city and palaces at the time.

Old masters: a room in the Picture Gallery on the upper floor

Leopold Museum

ADDRESS: MuseumsQuartier, Museumsplatz 1
OPENING TIMES: daily except Tuesday 10 a.m. to 7 p.m.,
Thursday 10 a.m. to 9 p.m.
GUIDED TOURS: group reservations available at
vermittlung@leopoldmuseum.org. Tours of the current special
exhibition are on Saturday, Sunday and holidays at 3 p.m. and
on Thursday at 7 p.m.
PHONE: +43/1/52570-0
INTERNET: www.leopoldmuseum.org
E-MAIL: office@leopoldmuseum.org

The collection of the Viennese ophthalmologist Rudolf
Leopold, which he assembled between the years 1947 and
1994 and which is now in the possession of the Republic

of Austria, amounts to approximately 5300 objects. The emphasis is on Austrian art of the 19th century (Georg Ferdinand Waldmüller, Anton Romako, Emil Jakob Schindler) and the first half of the 20th century. The Egon Schiele collection, with 47 paintings and almost 200 graphic works, is the largest in the world. Some of these exhibits, such as "Selbstseher" (Self-Seer; 1911), "Der Lyriker" (The Lyric Poet; 1911), "Kardinal und Nonne" (Cardinal and Nun; 1912), "Selbstbildnis mit Judenkirschen" (Self-Portrait with Winter-Cherries; 1912), "Eremiten" (Hermit; 1912) and "Entschwebung" (Floating Away; 1915) rank among Schiele's most important works. Little wonder that the museum chose as its logo the silhouette of a male nude, part of a work from the year 1910.

The collection also features masterpieces by Albin Egger Lienz, Oskar Kokoschka, Alfred Kubin, Gustav Klimt, Richard Gerstl, Herbert Boeckl and Anton Kolig. It is supplemented by arts and crafts objects as well as furniture by Otto Wagner, Adolf Loos, Josef Hoffmann, Koloman Moser und Dagobert Peche. Also on display are authentic objects from sub-Saharan Africa and Oceania as well as examples of Chinese and Japanese art that illustrate the influence of these styles on the ornamental art of Jugendstil (Austrian Art Nouveau). Only a few international examples of Expressionism are included (Edvard Munch, Ernest Ludwig Kirchner and Georges Rouault). About 1200 pieces are on permanent display: 600 of the 880 paintings, 100 of more than 3000 graphic works and 500 of the 1400 objects.

Tour: The museum with its almost square ground plan (40 by 45 meters; 127 by 143 feet) is accessible via a broad outside staircase in the Main Courtyard of the MuseumsQuartier. After passing through the entrance hall with the box office, the visitor enters a central, 21-meter-high (69 feet) atrium that is flooded with light. Its walls, like the exterior of the building, are lined with white Vraza limestone (Danube shell limestone from Bulgaria). The rectangular halls are arranged around the atrium and a second, lower-lying atrium like the blades of a windmill. Thus a direction of motion is set for the visitor in which three levels of the building can be visited continuously, without need to backtrack or enter a room twice.

The museum is nearly a cube, with two-thirds of its height (24 meters; 76 feet) rising from the inner courtyard of the MuseumsQuartier and the bottom third (13 meters, 41

Rudolf Leopold and the Foundation

Numerous important art collectors lived in Vienna until the seizure of power by Adolf Hitler in March 1938. The most important among them were Alphonse Rothschild, Prince Franz Josef II of Liechtenstein, the industrial magnate Ferdinand Bloch-Bauer, the librettist Fritz Grünbaum as well as the dentist Heinrich Rieger, who treated the destitute Egon Schiele in exchange for pictures. All of them were forced to emigrate or were murdered in the concentration camps. The tradition of upper-middle-class patronage was generally not continued after World War II and few private collectors emerged. Among the few who did, Rudolf Leopold stood out from the rest. By the mid-1980s, his collection – primarily of Austrian art from the Biedermeier period to Expressionism – illustrated the deficiencies of the Austrian state collections.

Rudolf Leopold was born in Vienna in 1925, studied medicine in the post-war years, received his medical degree in 1953, and finally specialized in ophthalmology. In 1947 he began to attend lectures on art history and to collect works of the 19th century. At an auction in 1950, he happened upon a forgotten catalogue of Egon Schiele's works, which had been published by the art dealer Otto Kallir-Nirenstein. Until 1938, Kallir-Nirenstein had exhibited at his Neue Gallerie pictures by the most important Austrian artists of the modern period. Rudolf Leopold was excited by the radical visual language of Schiele, whose art had been labeled "pornographic" in his own day. Leopold cared little about the lack of interest that the international art world showed for Schiele and the disparaging opinion that most art historians held of his work. He acquired practically every work of Schiele he could lay his hands on.

Leopold's passion for collecting, which was shared by his wife, Elisabeth, grew ever larger, sometimes bordering on fanaticism. In addition, he expanded the focus of his collection to Jugendstil, the period between the world wars, and after World War II. Leopold took out considerable bank loans, securing them with masterpieces. His spacious home in the Viennese suburb of Grinzing slowly turned into an art warehouse. Thousands of drawings were stored on cabinets and under

Rudolf and Elisabeth Leopold

beds, and multiple layers of paintings leaned against the walls. Because his house was filled far beyond capacity and the mountain of debt had assumed dangerous levels, Leopold considered selling his collection to the Republic of Austria. On the occasion of the exhibition Egon Schiele and His Time, Chancellor Franz Vranitzky announced in March 1989 that negotiations for the acquisition of the collection would be initiated.

For a long time the negotiations failed to produce a satisfying result: Leopold's expectations far exceeded the amount that had been considered by the government. Furthermore, Leopold was not willing to have his collection added to the holdings of a museum of Austrian modern art: he wanted to see his life's work preserved as a whole. Hans Dichand, the publisher of the newspaper *Kronen Zeitung*, turned out to be a powerful ally. The widely read daily repeatedly called for the purchase of the collection.

In 1992 the *Kronen Zeitung*, together with the Freedom Party, launched a huge campaign against construction of the planned MuseumsQuartier. Even with all the downsizing, the project did not seem feasible. Erhard Busek, at that time minister of science, solved the conundrum by linking the two projects: in October 1993 the government decided to establish a Leopold Museum in the MuseumsQuartier, which to a certain extent owes its existence to Rudolf Leopold. Leopold had rejected the idea of housing his collection in the Baroque wing of the Imperial Stables. Instead, he insisted on a new building. Even the *Kronen Zeitung* had to accept this, and in the spring of 1994, planning resumed.

The negotiations between Busek and Leopold must have been rather nerve-racking for both sides. To establish an accurate value of the collection and the exact number of artworks, two experts were entrusted with drawing up an inventory and estimate. They arrived at a total of approximately 574 million euros for 5266 objects. This appraisal was not completely accurate, because it was based on the expected price of each artwork sold individually. The auction of the collection as a whole could scarcely have achieved that price.

In the early summer of 1994, an agreement was reached: Leopold agreed to transfer the entire collection to a foundation. In return he would receive 160 million euros in a series of annual, indexed partial payments until May 2007. Furthermore it was agreed that Leopold would hold for life the director's position of the museum bearing his name. He also had the right to name four of the eight board members of his foundation. With that, Parliament voted to purchase the collection, and in August 1994 the charter of the foundation was signed. Soon after the collection was moved from Leopold's home to the MuseumsQuartier, where a temporary high-security storage facility had been built, Leopold began assembling his "Collection II." It includes not only works by Schiele, Klimt and Kokoschka, but also acquisitions down to the present (Günter Brus, Otto Mühl and Hermann Nitsch).

Being director of the museum gave Leopold the opportunity to play an active role in the detailed planning of the building. He fought for every floor, for every square meter. In March 1997 the draft design was submitted and in May 1999 the cornerstone was laid. In September 2001, scarcely three months after the official opening of the MuseumsQuartier, the Leopold Museum opened as well.

feet) underground. It encompasses five storeys and another two intermediate levels on which the shop, café and information lounge are located. The entrance level and the two upper levels are dedicated to 20th-century art. Nineteenth-century art is exhibited on the two lower levels, which also house a 117-seat auditorium and the magazine (not open to the public). Management, administration and workshops found a home in the adjacent existing building.

The entrance level serves as a symbolic threshold between the 19th and 20th centuries and exhibits works of Viennese Jugendstil by members of the Secession, foremost among them Gustav Klimt, and representatives of the Wiener

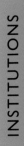

Werkstätte such as Josef Hoffmann and Koloman Moser. Works by the loner Richard Gerstl complete the presentation. Next chronologically come the exhibits of the top floor. Works by Anton Faistauer, Anton Kolig, Hans Boehler, Herbert Boeckl, Lovis Corinth, Ernest Ludwig Kirchner, Oskar Kokoschka and Albert Paris Guetersloh are featured along with the world's largest collection of paintings by Egon Schiele. The panoramic window offers a wonderful view of

Egon Schiele: "Seated Nude with Green Headscarf" (1914).

the city center and the MuseumsQuartier.

A highlight is provided on the second storey by two halls displaying the paintings of Albin Egger-Lienz and pictures by Maria Lassnig and Oswald Oberhuber that serve as a connection between the post-war period and the present. Paintings by Josef Dobrowsky, Alfons Walde, Gustav Hessing and other artists can be seen as well. Rudolf Leopold wants to raise awareness for "artists who have been unduly forgotten or are unknown to today's public" by the presentation of their work within the context of Schiele, Klimt and Kokoschka.

On display on the first basement level are 19th-century paintings by artists that include Ferdinand Georg Waldmüller, Friedrich Gauermann, Michael Neder, August von Pettenkofen, Anton Romako, Emil Jacob Schindler, Tina Blau, Olga Wisinger-Florian and Carl Schuch. The second basement level accommodates light-sensitive graphic works, including some by Gustav Klimt, Egon Schiele and Alfred Kubin, and it is also used for special exhibitions.

Egon Schiele: "Self-Portrait with Winter-Cherries" (1912).

Lipizzaner Museum

ADDRESS: Stallburg, Reitschulgasse 2
OPENING TIMES: daily 9 a.m. to 6 p.m.
GUIDED TOURS: Saturday at noon
PHONE: +43/1/525 24-583
INTERNET: www.lipizzaner.at
E-MAIL: lipizzaner@khm.at

Since 1997, the rooms of the former Hofapotheke (Imperial Court Pharmacy, 1746–1991) in the southwestern corner of the Stallburg have housed the Lipizzaner Museum. A permanent exhibition mounted by the ➤ **Kunsthistorisches Museum** as a joint project with the ➤ **Spanish Riding School** explains the history, breeding and training of the famous horses from the 16th century to the present. The tour takes us from the former sales room (now the Museum Shop and under preservation order) through the basement, where the medicinal wines were formerly stored. It begins with information about the famous Spanish Horses as well as the stud at Lipica (Lipizza) and covers such themes as riding skills, the Winterreitschule (Winter Riding Hall) and celebrations at court. Among the exhibits are drawings, photographs and sculptures as well as oil paintings by Johann Georg von Hamilton, who painted the favorite horses of Emperor Charles VI, and copperplate engravings by Johann Elias Ridinger. The Spanish Riding School has provided uniforms, harnesses, magnificent saddle cloths and studbooks. Large-screen monitors show the Lipizzaner horses, whose stables are right next door.

The former Imperial Court Pharmacy (below). Johann Georg von Hamilton: "Neput, the Horse of Emperor Charles VI" (above)

Museum of Modern Art
Ludwig Foundation Vienna

ADDRESS: MuseumsQuartier, Museumsplatz 1
OPENING TIMES: Tuesday to Sunday 10 a.m. to 6 p.m.,
Thursday 10 a.m. to 9 p.m.
LIBRARY: Tuesday to Thursday 10 a.m. to 3:30 p.m.
GUIDED TOURS (overall view): Sunday at 2 p.m. (in German)
PHONE: +43/1/525 00
INTERNET: www.mumok.at
E-MAIL: info@mumok.at or kunstvermittlung@mumok.at

The Museum of Modern Art with its rectangular ground plan and its façade of rough, dark basalt rock is as much the opposite of the Leopold Museum in appearance as it is in its holdings. While the ➤ **Leopold Museum** concentrates on Austrian art since the Biedermeier period, the Museum of Modern Art specializes in international art of the 20th century to the present.

The collection is built around a core of Fluxus and Nouveau Réalisme (formerly the Hahn Collection) and Pop Art and Photorealism (the Ludwig Collection). Also of note are the holdings of Arte Povera, Minimal Art, Land Art and Deconstructivism. In addition, during the 1990s an extensive collection of Central and Eastern European art was assembled. Classic modernism (Expressionism, Cubism) is represented by only a few examples. No other museum, however, has as many masterpieces of Viennese Actionism, which is considered to be the most important contribution of Austria to avant-garde art. In total, the holdings of the Museum of Modern Art number about 7000 objects.

History: In February 1958, Heinrich Drimmel, the People's Party (ÖVP) minister of education at the time, announced his intention to establish a museum for contemporary art in Vienna. "For the time being" it was to be accommodated in the Austria Pavilion built for the World's Fair in Brussels, a structure for which a suitable use was sought. In 1959, the art historian Werner Hofmann was given responsibility for establishing the museum and assembling the collection. The Museum des 20. Jahrhunderts (Museum of the 20th Century) opened in September 1962 near the South Station with the exhibition Art from 1900 to Today. Two-thirds of the 328 works shown were on loan. A detailed and balanced collection could no longer

Enormous machine: the Museum's light and lift shaft

be acquired: despite skillful purchasing, many gaping holes in the collection (e.g. Expressionism, Cubism, Neue Sachlichkeit) could not be closed in the decades that followed.

In the spring of 1977, the Wiener Künstlerhaus presented the exhibition Art Around 1970, which was a selection from the collection of Irene and Peter Ludwig, a German chocolate manufacturer. Stylistically, the emphasis was on Pop Art and Photo Realism. Subsequently, negotiations began, with the goal of securing loans for a museum of modern art in Vienna. Agreement was reached with Peter Ludwig in February 1978. But he issued an ultimatum to the Republic of Austria: he would make approximately 120 works available, but only if a suitable home could be found within one year for the new collection, which also would include objects from the Museum of the 20th Century. First an extension of the World's Fair Pavilion was considered, but a location in the Messepalast was discussed as well. Then, however, the Liechtenstein royal family offered its Baroque palace in Vienna's 9th district, which had been the home of its art collection until 1945.

With the additional building, which was opened in April 1979, the institution was reorganized as the Museum of Modern Art, which consisted organizationally and conceptually of the two houses. The goal by that time was to combine the two collections in a suitable building in the former Imperial Stables.

While the preparations for the first exhibition were underway, negotiations had come to a standstill between the City of Cologne and Wolfgang Hahn, then the chief restorer of the Wallraff Richartz Museum, over the purchase of the latter's art collection. Hertha Firnberg (Socialist Party), who was science minister at the time, reacted quickly, purchasing in 1978 approximately 400 works with an emphasis on Fluxus and Nouveau Réalisme for the Museum of Modern Art. This enormous addition suddenly gave the collection an almost completely new face.

The Ludwigs immediately communicated their willingness to donate the artworks that were on loan. In January 1981, the Österreichische Ludwig Stiftung für Kunst und Wissenschaft (Austrian Ludwig Foundation for Art and Science) was created. On condition that the Republic of Austria would create a fund for expanding the collection and transfer to it 10 million schillings (726,000 euros) each year for 15 years, they agreed to donate 129 works. The Ludwigs made a second donation in 1991. The funding agreement was extended to 30 years (until 2021), and the name of the institution changed to Museum Moderner Kunst: Stiftung Ludwig Wien (Museum of Modern Art Ludwig Foundation Vienna). This arrangement has made important purchases possible every year (including works by Paul Klee, Francis Bacon, Gerhard Richter, Michelangelo Pistoletto, Mario Merz and Andy Warhol).

From the first phase of the architectural competition (1986), the Museum has been an essential part of the MuseumsQuartier. Nevertheless, its inclusion was challenged several times. In addition, several space reductions had to be endured. In January 1993, pressured by a citizens' action group instigated by the newspaper *Kronen Zeitung* and the Freedom Party, the building volume had to be reduced by 20 percent. A whole floor was lost in March 1995. Construction of the MuseumsQuartier started in April 1998. The new building opened in September 2001.

Existential: a sculpture by Alberto Giacometti

Tour: An outside staircase ten meters (31 feet) wide leads to the entrance level, four meters (13 feet) above the level of the MQ Main Courtyard and vertically aligned with the center of the building. Two main exhibition levels are above the entrance level, two below. A 35-meter (111-foot) high atrium, which is illuminated from above, cuts the museum across all levels into two differently proportioned space groups. On one side are five exhibition levels, each with approximately 700 m^2 (7500 square feet) of floor space five meters (16 feet) high. On the other side are the more intimate "cabinets" 3.5 meters (11 feet) high.

The arrangement of space is not immediately obvious to the visitor. In addition, it is not possible to tour the building in a logical sequence of rooms. Upon entering, it becomes immediately obvious, however, that this museum is an enormous machine from a time long past. This impression is created by the materials used (cast iron for the stairs and wall linings; glass and basalt lava), and the central shaft with the three elevator systems and the bridges that lead to the exhibition halls. The architectural concept of the huge shaft has been massively impaired since June 2002 by a white, tunnel-like bridge. This intervention by Heimo Zobernig created a direct connection between two exhibition halls, which have been used for changing exhibitions ever since.

The most sensible course of action is to approach the museum from the top floor: the imposing Cupola Hall with its panoramic window is flooded with daylight and has a gallery that primarily features exhibitions related to the permanent collection. The level beneath is dedicated to special exhibitions. The best way of accessing the other areas of the museum is by walking down the staircase and taking a look inside each doorway as it presents itself. Thus one also arrives on the entrance level, which appears brutally cut into the shaft. The descent continues to exhibition Level 3 and finally to the "Factory" deep underground, reserved for young viewpoints and contemporary currents.

Towards the rear of the entrance level is the access to the shop and to the restaurant with its bar and reading lounge. The library, which is open to the public, can be reached via the adjacent "Spange." The separate conference hall "Hofstallung" is located in the Oval Wing of the MuseumsQuartier. It can be reached by means of a more recently built bridge along the rear of the museum.

Museum of Ethnology

ADDRESS: Neue Burg (Corps de Logis), Heldenplatz
REOPENING: early 2007
PHONE: +43/1/534 30-0
INTERNET: www.ethno-museum.ac.at
E-MAIL: v*@ethno-museum.ac.at

The most famous object in the Museum für Völkerkunde (Museum of Ethnology) is also one of the oldest and most fragile. It is a headdress made out of 450 tail feathers of the quetzal bird. There is a persistent rumor that it once belonged to the penultimate Aztec ruler, Montezuma, but that is not supported by the facts. In the late 16th century it was listed as a "Moorish hat" in the collection of Archduke Ferdinand in Ambras Castle in Tirol. Among the other holdings of international importance are the 238 artifacts brought back by the British explorer James Cook (1728–1779) from his three research expeditions around the world, the bronze statues from the Benin kingdom of West Africa (today Nigeria), and Johann Natterer's Brazilian Collection assembled between 1817 and 1835 with more than 2000 ethnographic items from over 60 various Indian tribes, most of which no longer exist or have lost their cultural identity.

Glass-roofed courtyard: the Corps de Logis in the Neue Burg

The best-known exhibit:
Aztec feather headdress from
the 16th century

History: In 1806 the Austrian naturalist Leopold von Fichtel was commissioned by Emperor Francis I to buy part of the collection of James Cook at auction in London. In the following decades, the holdings were enlarged by the addition of a number of other collections These included the Asian-Oceanic collection of Baron Karl von Hügel (1839) and the collection that had originated during the circumnavigation of the globe by the frigate *Novara* between 1857 and 1859. The main problem was the lack of a special museum: the artifacts were usually packed away in crates. In addition, compared with other departments of the Court Natural History Cabinet, the ethnographic collection did not have a specialized curator.

With the founding of the ➤ **Naturhistorisches Museum** in 1876, the stock of the anthropological-ethnographic collections found a permanent place at that institution. By 1918, the holdings had grown from fewer than 5000 to more than 94,000 objects. This expansion, however, led to a pressing shortage of space and thus to considerations about moving the ethnographic collections to the Corps de Logis. Since 1908, it had housed the collections assembled during the journey around the world by Francis Ferdinand, Archduke of Austria-Este (1892–93).

The transfer of the Ethnographic Department to the Emperor's guesthouse with its impressive glassed-over courtyard began in 1926; two years later the first show-rooms of the Ethnological Museum opened. The ➤ **Kunsthistorisches Museum** also began to spread successively into the Neue Burg: in 1935, the ➤ **Hofjagd- und Rüstkammer (Collection of Arms and Armour)** was set up. It was followed in 1947 by the ➤ **Sammlung alter Musikinstrumente (Collection of Ancient Musical Instruments)** and in 1978 by the ➤ **Ephesus Museum.** The Museum of Ethnology became part of the Kunsthistorisches Museum in 2002. Because the building is undergoing a complete overhaul that began in 1999, the Museum has been closed since the spring of 2004. Its collections currently contain around 240,000 objects, 72,000 photographs and 132,000 printed works.

Naturhistorisches Museum

ADDRESS: Burgring 7 (entrance: Maria-Theresien-Platz)
OPENING TIMES: daily except Tuesday 9 a.m. to 6:30 p.m.
(Wednesday 9 a.m. to 9 p.m.)
GUIDED HISTORICAL TOURS ALL THE WAY TO THE ROOF:
Wednesday 5 p.m. and 6:30 p.m., Sunday 2 p.m. and 4 p.m.
Insights into the museum's scientific research:
Saturday 2:30 p.m., Sunday 10:30 a.m.
EVENING EVENTS (guided tours, lectures): Wednesday 7 p.m.
Children's program: Saturday 2 p.m., Sunday 10 a.m. and 2 p.m.
PHONE: +43/1/521 77-0
INTERNET: www.nhm-wien.ac.at
E-MAIL: waswannwo@nhm-wien.ac.at

The Naturhistorisches Museum is a world unto itself:
only a fraction of its 20 million objects can be displayed,
and yet the great variety of beautifully presented displays
is still astonishing. In addition, there are times when you
feel as though you've entered another age: the furniture
and wooden display cases have remained unchanged since
the Museum opened in 1889. But there is a special quality
about this feeling of dustiness, of anachronism: the
Museum, which is one of the loveliest in Vienna, is also a
museum to the concept of museums.
The giant show-rooms cover a total area of 8700 m²
(94,000 square feet). Wandering through them, you con-
stantly stumble across some special item or curiosity: a

A museum to the concept of museums: the Geology-Paleontology Department

giant topaz weighing 117 kilograms (257 pounds) or an ostrich egg that is almost the size of a medicine ball, a silver bandfish with pink gills and a record length of 5.5 meters (18 feet) or the 4.8-meter (16-foot) long lower jawbone of a fin whale. The most important object, however, is the 25,000-year-old figurine of the "Venus of Willendorf," which has its own small room. And despite the thousands upon thousands of stuffed animals, the Naturhistorisches Museum never seems dead: in the basement, for example, is a vivarium with many separate areas for fish, birds and lizards. And visitors can use the Museum's microscopes to their heart's content. A guided tour to the roof is especially recommended.

History: In 1750 Emperor Francis I Stephen of Lorraine (1708–1765), the husband of Maria Theresa, acquired from the Florentine scholar Johann Ritter von Baillou what at that time was the biggest and most famous collection of natural-history objects in the world. It consisted of around 30,000 items, including rare fossils, snails, mussels and corals as well as minerals and precious stones. In contrast to many other Wunderkammer (natural wonders rooms) this collection had already been classified according to scientific criteria.

Francis Stephen, who also founded the Menagerie at Schönbrunn Palace in 1752 and the Botanical Garden a year later, also equipped Austria's first overseas scientific expedition. In 1755 Nicolaus Joseph Jacquin brought back

from his journey to the Caribbean, the Antilles, Venezuela and Colombia many living plants and animals as well 67 crates of natural wonders. Following the premature death of the Emperor, the collection became the property of the state. It was rearranged and put on public display two days a week. In 1776 Empress Maria Theresa, who took a great interest in the earth sciences as the basis of mining and industry,

Venus of Willendorf: 25,000 years old

invited the mineralogist Ignaz von Born to come to Vienna to organize and expand the collections. He began buying minerals of every provenance, and the natural-history cabinet became a center of practice-oriented research.

Emperor Francis II/I (1768–1835) added a cabinet of animals to the natural-science collection. The basic holdings were provided by the Habsburg's hunting trophies, which dated from the time of Emperor Maximilian II (1564–1576). After several reorganizations, a cabinet of plants was founded in 1807. The stuffed animals at that time were displayed in artificial landscape dioramas and thus within an ecological context. Next to them, however, were stuffed examples of people from foreign races, including the "Princely Moor" Angelo Soliman.

On the occasion of the marriage of his daughter Leopoldine to Pedro I of Brazil, Emperor Francis sent an expedition to that country in 1817. Two Austrian frigates accompanied the Archduchess to Rio de Janeiro. Among the participants on this voyage was the taxidermist Johann Natterer, who ended up spending 18 years in the rain forests of South America instead of the two years that he had planned. During his research travels he collected huge quantities of exotic animals, plants, minerals and ethnologic items. Because there was not enough room in the Hofburg for these objects, consideration was given to building a "Brazilian Museum."

The most ambitious expedition in the history of Austrian research was the circumnavigation of the globe by the frigate *Novara* (1857–1859). It was proposed by Archduke Ferdinand Maximilian, the commander of the Navy, who provided use of the ship for two years to the Academy of Sciences and the Geographic Society. The expedition came back with an enormous quantity of items. The last important research journey was the expedition to the North Pole by the *Tegetthoff* between 1872 and 1874. It was led by Julius von Payer and Karl Weyprecht, who discovered Franz Joseph Land on August 30, 1873.

Meanwhile, construction of a new Naturhistorisches Museum had become a necessity. In the plan for the Kaiserforum (Imperial Forum) by Gottfried Semper and Carl von Hasenauer, it was the mirror image of the ➤ **Kunsthistorisches Museum** (q.v. for the architectural history). In 1871 excavation began and on August 10, 1889, the Museum opened.

The 170-meter (560-foot) long and 70-meter (230-foot)

wide building was crowned by a drum cupola bearing a colossal bronze statue of the Greek sun god, Helios. On the lower and middle levels (Intermediate Floor and Upper Floor), the figural decoration of the façade consists of allegorical and mythological depictions of the Development of the World and of the Cosmos. On the balustrade stand 34 chalky-limestone statues of scientists from classical antiquity to the 19th century as signs of progress. The figures and decorations in the Cupola Hall and in the Staircase as well as the ceiling fresco "The Cycle of Life" by Hans Canon are based on similar themes. In the showrooms more than 100 oil paintings illustrate the places the objects were found, depicting primeval landscapes and distant lands.

The Ethnographic Department, whose holdings had grown tremendously, were separated from the rest of the objects and moved in 1926 to the Corps de Logis in the Neue Burg. Two years the ➤ **Museum of Ethnology** opened its first show-rooms. In 1990, a subterranean depot with four levels was built beneath the Naturhistorisches Museum. The attic was finished between 1991 and 1995.

Tour: The internal structure of the Museum is characterized by the strictly systematic arrangement of the displays. On the Hochparterre (Intermediate Floor) they range from the realm of inanimate nature to traces of life from ancient geological eras to human beings. The Ober-

Zoological Collection: 600 mammals, 3200 birds, 700 fish, etc.

geschoss (Upper Floor) presents diverse forms of animal life as well as the world of microscopic organisms. Within the individual areas of the collection, the objects are arranged systematically: either according to natural relationships or their chronological sequence.

The Collection of Minerals (Rooms 1–5) is one of the most important in the world. Among its distinctive items are Colombian emeralds, diamonds and nuggets of gold and platinum. The Collection of Meteorites has more than 700 objects and is the oldest and biggest of its kind. In the Geology-Paleontology Department (Rooms 6–10) there is a complete skeleton of a 17-million-year-old elephant called a *Deinotherium*, a huge fossil palm leaf, a three-toed horse called a *Mesohippus*, the gigantic perissodactyl *Chalicotherium* and a diorama of a tropical coral reef 16 million years ago. Among the most spectacular objects in the dinosaur room are the skeletons of an *Allosaurus*, an *Iguanodon* and a *Diplodocus*. The 4.5-meter (15-foot) length of the fossilized *Archelon* makes it the biggest sea turtle ever found.

The corridors of the Hochparterre (Intermediate Floor) are dedicated to the Ice Age. The Prehistoric Department (Rooms 11–15) presents archaeological material from the Old Stone Age to the early Middle Ages, including, along with the "Venus of Willendorf," also the "Fanny of Galgenberg," a cult statuette from Stratzing. The Anthropology Department (Room 16) documents the development of humankind on the basis of skulls from the Middle Stone Age, New Stone Age, Bronze Age, Hallstatt culture, Celts, Romans, Germans, Slavs and Avars over a period of 35,000 years.

The "Mikrotheater" has been installed in Room 21 on the second floor. During demonstrations, microorganisms are magnified several thousand times and projected on a screen, and they can even be viewed three-dimensionally (every Saturday and Sunday at 1:30, 3 and 4:15 p.m.). The Invertebrate Collection (Rooms 22 and 23) with its tremendous variety of mussels and snails, corals, worms and arachnids leads to the insects (Room 24). This special collection alone has ten million objects, and even the relatively small part of the collection on display is impressive: more than 50,000 butterflies, grasshoppers, bees, gnats, flies and beetles in 224 giant display cases. Most of the upper floor (Rooms 25–39) is dedicated to vertebrate animals. The Zoological Collection displays 600 mammals, 3200 birds,

700 fish and 500 reptiles. Because many of them have meanwhile become extinct, some of the stuffed animals, which are as much as 200 years old (including the dodo, great auk and the Tasmanian wolf), are priceless rarities.

Österreichische Nationalbibliothek (Austrian National Library): The Modern Library

ADDRESS: Neue Burg (Middle Gate), Heldenplatz
OPENING TIMES MAIN READING ROOM: Monday to Friday
9 a.m. to 9 p.m. (July to September, 9 a.m. to 4 p.m., closed
September 1–7), Saturday 9 a.m. to 12:45 p.m.
PHONE: +43/1/534 10-252
INTERNET: www.onb.ac.at

The service facilities of the Austrian National Library are located in the Neue Burg: the local loan and borrowing desks, the Main Reading Room and other reading rooms, the periodical department, the catalogues and databases. The Picture Archive is next door in the Corps de Logis (entrance ➤ **Museum of Ethnology**). The collections of the ANL currently hold around 7.3 million objects, including 8000 incunabula and more than three million printed works. The library is divided into ten special collections. Of outstanding international importance are not only the manuscripts (including the Golden Bull of 1356 and the 2400-page Wenceslas Bible) and musical manuscripts (including the *Requiem* by Wolfgang Amadeus

In the Neue Burg: the service facilities of the National Library

Mozart and Ludwig van Beethoven's *Violin Concerto*), but also the incunabula and other old printed books (a Gutenberg Bible), historical maps, portraits and photographs, posters, bookplates and handbills as well as the literary estates of Austrian authors (Robert Musil, Ingeborg Bachmann, Erich Fried and many others).

History: The building for the Court Library that was completed in 1726 (with the ➤ **Prunksaal** or State Hall by Johann Bernhard Fischer von Erlach) soon became too small, on the one hand because of the demand that everything of importance be preserved and, on the other hand, the growth that occurred when Joseph II ordered the closing of the monastery libraries. The Court Library spread into adjoining buildings, including the Augustinian monastery. At the beginning of the 20th century, underground stacks for books were built as much as 14 meters (46 feet) deep beneath Joseph's Square. In 1920, following the downfall of the monarchy, the Court Library became the National Library and ownership was transferred to the Republic of Austria. Since 1945 it has been known officially as the Austrian National Library.

Between 1962 and 1966, several reading rooms as well as the borrowing desk were established in the Neue Burg, and two collections were moved there (Department of Papyri and the Department of Broadsheets, Posters and Exlibris). Since 1992, the air-conditioned subterranean depot beneath the Burggarten has been in use, with room on four levels for around four million volumes. In an essay, Gerhard Roth describes the subterranean stacks of the ANL as a "book mine." With the library growing at an annual rate of around 50,000 volumes, the present storage capacity will remain sufficient only until 2010. Plans are being made for another subterranean depot (beneath Heldenplatz).

Since January 2002, the ANL has been managed along the same model as the Federal Museums as an independent, non-profit and scholarly institution. Modernization and renovation of the service facilities in the Neue Burg are underway (installation of new wiring and cabling in the reading rooms, doubling the number of research terminals, remodeling the borrowing desks, creating a copy center and a reading lounge). Since 2003 the entire printed collection from 1501 to the present has been retrievable via the Internet. A long-term project is to digitize the books and periodicals.

Österreichisches Theatermuseum (Austrian Theatre Museum)

Gustav Klimt:
"Nuda Veritas" (1899)

ADDRESS: Lobkowitzplatz 2
OPENING TIMES: Tuesday to Sunday
10 a.m. to 6 p.m.
PHONE: +43/1/512 88 00-610
INTERNET: www.theatermuseum.at
E-MAIL: info@theatermuseum.at

A visit to the Theatre Museum is anything but boring: Herbert Kappelmüller designed the tour on the second floor of Lobkowitz Palace to be a theatrical and entertaining production. You stroll across the cobblestones and come across an old advertising pillar with posters; you suddenly find yourself in an orchestra pit where the musicians are tuning their instruments; or you enter a photo lab to find trays of developer with old pictures floating in them. Rockets explode to the tune of fireworks music, and through the velvet-lined doors of the boxes you can look down on the stage (or on the stage models). In the cemetery-like memorial room with personal effects from estates, the gravel crunches beneath your feet.

The Theatre Museum has more than 1.6 million objects, including more than 100,000 sketches and drawings, almost 1000 architectural and stage models, over 700,000 photos and around 2000 souvenirs of famous actors, authors and composers. The oldest playbill in the collection dates from the year 1713 and is an announcement of a harlequinade. Among the autographs are originals by Beethoven, Goethe, Richard Wagner, Richard Strauss and Gustav Mahler. Gustav Klimt's painting "Nuda Veritas" came to the museum from Hermann Bahr's estate. In addition, there are many costumes, some of them designed by Oskar Kokoschka, Fritz Wotruba and Pablo Picasso, as well as marionettes and shadow figures. One room is dedicated to the Jugendstil artist Richard

Teschner (1879–1948) and his revolutionary rod-puppet theatre called Figurenspiegel (Figure Mirror). Evening performances are occasionally staged. The Library contains around 80,000 books and periodicals (open from Tuesday to Friday 10 a.m. to 1 p.m. and 2 p.m. to 4:45 p.m., on Saturday 10 a.m. to 1 p.m.). The memorial rooms at Hanusch-gasse 3 include tributes to Carl Michael Ziehrer, Emmerich Kálmán, Hugo Thimig, Hermann Bahr, Max Reinhardt, Caspar Neher and Fritz Wotruba (open by appointment).

History: The Theatre Museum was created in 1991 from the Theatre Collection of the ➤ **Österreichische National-bibliothek (Austrian National Library)**. While the Theatre Collection was not founded until 1922, it was based on several preliminary stages of collecting at the Court Library dating as far back as the Baroque period. As a result of an exhibition on comedy in the Library's State Hall, the extensive collection of Hugo Thimig, director of the Burgtheater, was purchased in 1923. In 1931 several rooms in the **Burgtheater** (➤ **Environs**) became available for the Federal Theatre Museum. The museum was closed, however, in 1938.

There has been a real Austrian Theatre Museum only since 1975. In 1982 a decision was made to combine the Theatre Collection of the National Library and the Theatre Museum. The obvious place to put it was Lobkowitz Palace, which had just been purchased by the Republic of Austria. The Theatre Collection was finally separated from the National Library, and the Theatre Museum acquired the status of a Federal Museum. It opened on October 26, 1991. A decade later the Theatre Museum lost its independence. At the beginning of 2001, it became

Theatralical presentation: varied historical costumes

Eroica Hall: ceiling painting by Jakob van Schuppen (around 1730)

part of the ➤ **Kunsthistorisches Museum**.

On a commission from Philipp Sigmund Count Dietrichstein, the architect Giovanni Pietro Tencala began planning Lobkowitz Palace in 1687. It was built between 1690 and 1694 with the participation of Johann Bernhard Fischer von Erlach, who designed the central projection, portal and attic. In 1745, the Baroque palace came into the possession of the Lobkowitz family. Prince Francis Joseph Maximilian Prince of Lobkowitz was an important patron of the music and theatre scene of that time. Himself a musician and later director of the Court Theatre, he built a concert hall in 1799. Ludwig van Beethoven often played at the palace and among the numerous works that he dedicated to the Prince was his *Third Symphony*, composed in 1804 and originally entitled *Bonaparte*. In Beethoven's honor the concert hall is called the Eroica Hall today. In 1807 Beethoven's *Fourth Symphony* was given its première at Lobkowitz Palace, and in December 1812, the Gesellschaft der Musikfreunde (Society of the Friends of Music – Musikverein) was founded there. From 1869 on, the palace was rented to various tenants, including the French and the Czech embassies. After World War II it was rented to the French Cultural Institute. Since 1979 it has been the property of the Republic of Austria. The renovation and conversion to create the Theatre Museum took from 1985 to 1991.

Papyrus Museum

ADDRESS: Neue Burg (Middle Gate), Heldenplatz
OPENING TIMES: Monday and Wednesday to Friday
10 a.m. to 5 p.m. (July to September 10 a.m. to 4 p.m.)
PHONE: +43/1/534 10-425
INTERNET: www.onb.ac.at/sammlungen/papyrus/
E-MAIL: papyrus@onb.ac.at

The Papyrus Collection of the ➤ Österreichische Nationalbibliothek (Austrian National Library) is the largest of its
kind in the world. It holds around 138,000 papyri (from
the 15th century BC to the 16th century AD), more than
50,000 archaeological documents and 17,000 photographs.
The 400 most interesting objects are presented in a permanent exhibition on the basement floor of the Neue Burg
(entrance via the Modern Library). The 30 display cases
present ten different themes, including school, magic, the
hereafter, literature, the military and the police. Among the
objects on display are the oldest surviving "police ticket"
(issued because an old coat was discarded in the street) and
a recipe for toothpaste from the 4th century AD. It was
made of a dram each of rock salt and iris, two drams of
mint and 30 peppercorns. Various processes are also
explained, including the technique of writing on papyrus
with a reed pen and methods for preserving the fragments.

History: About 95 percent of the holdings in the Papyrus
Collection date back to the
private collection of Archduke Rainer, a nephew of
Emperor Francis Joseph. In
the Winter of 1878–79,
Egyptian agricultural labor-
ers searching for fertile soil
had dug up a sand dune
where they discovered the
refuse dump of the ancient
city of Crocodilopolis. The

Parchment fragment: "ticket" issued
because someone discarded an old
coat in the street

papyrus fragments they found made their way to the
antique market of Cairo, where they were discovered by
the Viennese antiquities dealer Theodor Graf. He
informed Josef von Karabacek, Professor of Oriental Languages at Vienna University, and the latter was able to
awaken the interest of Archduke Rainer. In 1883, the first
bundle of around 10,000 papyri was acquired. In 1899,
after making further purchases, the Archduke gave the

collection, which in part had been subjected to prior study and presented in an exhibition, to the Emperor as a gift to the Court Library.

Präsidentschaftskanzlei (Offices of the Austrian President)

Ostentatious suite:
the apartments of Maria Theresa

ADDRESS: Ballhausplatz
ADMISSION: only on special open days with permission.
PHONE: +43/1/53 422
INTERNET: www.hofburg.at

In 1920, after the downfall of the monarchy, the Office of the Federal President was instituted. Until 1938, the head of state had his offices in what is now the Federal Chancellery on Ballhausplatz. Because these rooms had been heavily damaged during World War II, the Presidential Offices were moved in 1946 with Russian permission to the Leopoldine Wing of the Hofburg, immediately across from the former Geheime Hofkanzlei (Secret Chancellery). The previous December, the Socialist Karl Renner had been elected the first president of Austria's Second Republic. The two parallel suites of rooms were once the apartments of Maria Theresa and Joseph II, respectively. When the President is present, the Austrian flag is hoisted on the roof.

Tour: The rooms adapted by Maria Theresa in the Leopoldine Wing, which had been completed in 1681, have generally kept the names they had in her day. On the courtyard side the Adlerstiege (Eagle Stairway) provides access to the First and Second Bellaria Rooms (Bellariazimmer). They got their name from the Bellaria ramp that Maria

Theresa installed in order to reach her apartments without having to climb stairs. The projection we see today on the narrow side of the building, the "Bellaria Gate," was not built until the second half of the 19th century.

In the Rosenzimmer, named for the rose ornament above the doors, is the Kaiserliche Vorstellungsuhr (Imperial Performance Clock), a mechanical clock that Maria Theresa received as a gift in 1750. It is considered one of the finest and most beautiful timepieces of the Baroque period and weighs 128 kilograms (282 pounds). The "performance" in the name takes place on a stage beneath the dial. Set in motion by a complicated mechanism, it pays homage to the imperial couple, Francis and Maria Theresa. The first room that was used for official functions is the Pietra-dura-Zimmer, named for the 67 mosaic pictures on the walls. They were assembled in Florence between 1737 and 1767 from colored semi-precious stones carefully cut to shape. This collection is by far the biggest in the world. The cabinets and tables are also of Florentine pietra-dura (literally "hard stone") work. The most beautiful table, however, is missing: during the Nazi period, the Italian foreign minister, Count Galeazzo

The President's reception room: the Empress died here in 1780

Ciano, presented it as a gift to the Gauleiter ("district leader") of Vienna, Baldur von Schirach.

The Miniaturenkabinett (Cabinet of Miniatures), which adjoins the Spiegelsaal (Hall of Mirrors), was Maria Theresa's study and contained her delicate escritoire. The room got its name from a collection of miniatures acquired by Maria Theresa's grandson Francis I. Many are images of members or relatives of the Imperial household.

The Maria Theresa Room was the Empress's bedroom after the death of her husband, and here she died in 1780 at the age of 63. The walls were hung with dark-red, gold-embroidered velvet. In the middle of the long wall stood her impressive bed with a heavy velvet canopy hung above it. Today the room is used by the President for receptions, for swearing in the government and for state visits. A tall astronomical clock is the most impressive piece in the room. Made in 1671, it is supposed to keep accurate time until 2160. The dial showing the local time has hands that move counter-clockwise, with the three on the left and the nine on the right. There was good reason for this: instead of having to turn to see the clock when she was lying in bed – where she often conducted state business – the Empress could see the time in a mirror across the room. When the room was restored in 1957, a niche was found to contain an altar. It is believed to have been built for Pope Pius VI, who visited Joseph II in 1782 to encourage him to adopt more lenient policies toward the monasteries.

The other adjoining rooms facing the courtyard were not part of Maria Theresa's apartments. The first, called the Jagdzimmer (Hunting Room), is now the conference room of the President. The suite of rooms facing Heldenplatz served as living quarters for Joseph II and were not nearly as lavish as those of his mother. The first room, the closest to the Swiss Court (Schweizerhof), was the Emperor's bedroom. Because of the color of the upholstery, it was called the Blue Salon. The next room, the Green Salon, was Joseph II's study and is now used by the President for the same purpose. An office area adjoins it. At the western end of the Leopoldine Wing is the almost unknown Josefskapelle (Joseph's Chapel), which Maria Theresa remodeled in 1772. A "closet door" allowed the Empress to enter the oratory without having to leave her apartment.

Prunksaal (State Hall) of the Austrian National Library

ADDRESS: Joseph's Square 1
OPENING TIMES: daily 10 a.m. to 2 p.m. Thursday 10 a.m. to
7 p.m. Starting January 2005: daily except Monday 10 a.m. to
6 p.m., Thursday 10 a.m. to 9 p.m.
PHONE: +43/1/534 10-397
INTERNET: www.onb.ac.at/siteseeing/prunksaal/

Don't be put off by the soberly decorated rooms on the
ground floor, which used to be stables and are now used
for events staged by the ➤ Österreichische Nationalbibliothek (Austrian National Library). The State Hall on the
second floor of the former Court Library is a Baroque
Gesamtkunstwerk (total work of art) with Daniel Gran's
ceiling frescoes, white marble statues by the brothers Paul
and Peter Strudel and walnut bookcases, and it is also one
of the most impressive library rooms in the world.
Designed by Johann Bernhard Fischer von Erlach, it has
extremely clear and attractive proportions: the room,
which opens in the middle to an oval space topped by a
cupola, is exactly 240 Wiener Schuh (Viennese feet) long

(77.7 meters, 255 feet) and 45 wide (14.6 meters, 48 feet). The height of the barrel vault is 60 Viennese feet (19 meters, 64 feet), the top of the dome 90 (29 meters, 96 feet). Around 200,000 volumes, mainly works from 1501 to 1850, are kept in the State Hall. The frescoes in the entrance wing are based on themes of the World and War. Those in the rear wing adjoining the Hofburg (with the entrance for the Emperor) are allegorical depictions of the Sky and Peace. In the dome is the *Apotheosis of Charles VI*, the builder of the Court Library, and the history of its construction.

Clear proportions: the State Hall by Johann Bernhard Fischer von Erlach

History: The origins of the former Court Library date from the late 14th century. The book considered to be the "founding volume" is the "Gospel Book of Johannes von Troppau" ordered by Duke Albert III and completed in 1368. It is written in gold letters and decorated in the Bohemian style of book illumination. It is the oldest book authenticated as a Habsburg-Austrian codex. The library experienced a big upswing under the direction of the Dutch scholar Hugo Blotius, who was hired in 1575 by Maximilian II to be the first official Court Librarian. A lack of space in the Minorite Monastery, where the library was housed from 1558 to 1623, forced a transfer to a building on the outer Burgplatz (Castle Square), where it remained until 1727.

In 1660, Leopold I planned to add a library storey to the riding-school building on the Tummelplatz (Exercise Ground) to the southeast of the Hofburg. But the plans drawn up in 1663 were not implemented until 1681. In 1683 the almost finished building was severely damaged during the Turkish siege, and it was apparently never repaired. In 1722, Johann Bernhard Fischer von Erlach began building the new Court Library on the foundations of the old riding-school building. His son Joseph Emanuel Fischer completed the structure in 1726, and Daniel Gran worked until 1730 to finished the wall and ceiling frescoes. Some 15,000 volumes of the recently acquired library of Prince Eugene of Savoy were installed in the central oval of the State Hall.

The foundations, however, proved inadequate and the dome threatened to collapse. From 1765 to 1767, Nikolaus Pacassi undertook measures to secure the building. The Main Staircase was rebuilt on a different design between 1767 and 1769. At the same time, Franz Anton Maulbertsch restored the damaged frescoes. Subsequently the Augustinian Wing and the façades of the side wings were built by Pacassi, who adapted them to harmonize with the architecture of the Court Library.

In 1829, the Late-Baroque Library Hall – with a 1775 ceiling fresco by Johann Bergl – of the adjoining Augustinian monastery was rented as storage space for books and copperplate engravings. From 1903 to 1906, it was remodeled to create the Augustinian Reading Room. It is not possible to simply visit this hall, which since 1995 has been the reading room of the Department of

The Library of Prince Eugene of Savoy

In 1737, a year after the death of Prince Eugene of Savoy, Emperor Charles VI purchased the famous Bibliotheca Eugeniana from the niece and heiress of the celebrated military commander. He paid the princess an annual pension of 10,000 florins, which proved to be an enormous sum because Victoria of Savoy lived another 26 years. The value of the library, which was housed in Prince Eugene's town palace on Himmelpfortgasse (today the Finance Ministry), was estimated to be "only" 150,000 florins.

The library comprised 15,000 printed works, 500 volumes and boxes of copperplate engravings and 240 precious manuscripts, which Prince Eugene – according to the poet Jean-Baptiste Rousseau – did not collect for ostentatious purposes but rather because he was a true friend of science, fine books and art. In addition to the personal interests and connections of the prince, the library also reflects the universal spectrum of fields of knowledge to be found in a princely library.

The books, which were uniformly bound in morocco leather, have the coat of arms of their owner stamped in gold on the front and back. The various fields of knowledge are distinguished by the color of the binding (history and literature in red, theology and law in blue, natural sciences in yellow/ochre). Among the most precious objects in the Bibliotheca Eugeniana is the "Tabula Peutingeriana" (Peutinger Table, a copy of a Roman map and now in the manuscript collection), the *Atlas Bleau van der Hem* (in the map collection) and a *Bible moralisée* with 2000 medallion illustrations.

Incunabula, Old and Precious Books. (Opening times: October to June, Monday, Wednesday and Friday 9 a.m. to 3:45 p.m. Tuesday and Thursday 9 a.m. to 7 p.m.; July to September, Monday to Friday 9 a.m. to 3:45 p.m., closed September 1–7.)

"quartier21"

ADDRESS: MuseumsQuartier, Museumsplatz 1
OPENING times of the theme streets Electric Avenue and
"transeuropa": daily from 10 a.m.
INTERNET: http://quartier21.mqw.at
E-MAIL: quartier21@mqw.at

"quartier21" encompasses all the spaces in the
MuseumsQuartier that are not permanently assigned
to institutions (a total of 4900 m², 53,000 square
feet). It includes the publicly accessible theme streets
Electric Avenue and "transeuropa" (including the
meeting areas of the Oval Hall and Erste Bank Arena)
as well as cultural offices and conference rooms in the
Fischer von Erlach Wing and several institutions
spread across the grounds.

History: In 1993 a number of small autonomous culture
institutions and associations began to establish offices
in the former Messepalast. They were assigned performance space free of charge, which they were allowed to
use until the MuseumsQuartier was built. With their
various activities, they helped enliven the run-down
area. Eventually, this made it politically impossible to
abandon the project MuseumsQuartier or the concept
of a multifunctional art and cultural center. Some ini-

Designer merchandise, fashions, CDs: Electric Avenue in "quartier21"

tially provisory organizations, such as the ➤ **Architek-turzentrum Wien** and the ➤ **Zoom Kindermuseum**, quickly established themselves on a permanent basis. Others remained temporary, were forced to disband due to insufficient funding and subsidies, or moved away. Now that renovation of the old buildings is complete, for the sake of flexibility the MuseumsQuartier Company usually grants leases with a term of only two years. "quartier21" opened in September 2002 with approximately 30 partner organizations.

Tour: The ground floor of the Fischer von Erlach Wing is laid out in such a way that visitors can wander the entire length of the building (if no events are being staged). "transeuropa" begins in the south with an open space, which is available for exhibitions of all kinds. Next to it is the "A9-forum transeuropa," in which the provinces that make up the Federal Republic of Austria present projects to introduce themselves. The core "transeuropa" space follows, with interlocked booths leased to various cultural organizations. Above the Oval Hall, the Main Entrance with MQ Point Info, the cultural bookshop Prachner and the Kantine (cafeteria), one can reach Electric Avenue. The partner organizations focus on electronic music (Cheap Records & Store), with video art, fashion and design. Electric Avenue ends at the northeast entrance of the MuseumsQuartier.
In addition to the Architekturzentrum, the Staatsratshof (State Councilor's Courtyard) also contains the "forum experimentelle architektur" and "basis wien." This information center, which is dedicated to current art, opened in July 1997 in the MuseumsQuartier, but moved in 2001 to Fünfhausgasse 5. The space in the MQ is still used as an "infopool" for exhibitions and events. Opening times: Tuesday to Sunday 2 p.m. to 7 p.m. (Internet: www.basis-wien.at). The two outside staircases in the Main Courtyard and the entrance on Breite Gasse lead to the attic of the Oval Wing, which is home to the mathematics laboratory "math.space." It offers regular workshops and lectures for pupils of all age groups. Opening times: Monday 10 a.m. to noon, Friday 3 p.m. to 5 p.m. (Internet: http://math.space.or.at).

Redoutensäle

ADDRESS: Joseph's Square
ADMISSION: only to public events
PHONE: +43/1/587 36 66
INTERNET: www.hofburg.com
E-MAIL: kongresszentrum@hofburg.com

Between 1744 and 1748, Jean-Nicolas Jadot built two ballrooms, the Kleiner and Grosser Redoutensaal, to replace the Dancing Hall originally constructed between 1629 and 1631. It had previously been converted into a theatre in 1652 and was adapted again in 1660 for

The Redoutensaal Wing in flames: the cause of the blaze is still unknown

The 1992 Fire in the Hofburg

On November 27, 1992, shortly after one o'clock in the morning, a night watchman discovered a fire in the Grosser Redoutensaal. The first fire engine arrived within three minutes, but soon the attic was in flames. While 240 firemen fought the blaze, police blocked off the city center. At around 2:30 a.m. the ceiling of the Grosser Redoutensaal collapsed. A half hour later the attic of the entire building was alight. Thousands of books were removed from the State Hall of the National Library, and 69 Lipizzaner horses were taken to safety in the Volksgarten. Fortunately, the fire did not spread to the library or the stables.

By 8:15 a.m. on November 28, the fire had been extin-

operatic performances. In 1759, a decade after the Redoutensäle were complete, Empress Maria Theresa commissioned Nikolaus Pacassi to remodel the two halls for the wedding of Joseph II and Isabella of Parma, and he added Late-Baroque stucco decorations.

The halls were the venue for numerous "Redouten" (masked balls), banquets, operatic performances and concerts: Ludwig van Beethoven's *Eighth Symphony* received its première in the Grosser Redoutensaal, Niccolò Paganini performed there in 1828, and the composers Josef Strauss and Franz Liszt conducted their works there as well. The

guished, but about three percent of the Hofburg complex had been damaged. The most serious destruction was in the Grosser Redoutensaal: the historical stucco ceiling was destroyed, and the Baroque structure of the attic was gone. In the Kleiner Redoutensaal the fire destroyed a third of the stucco ceiling. The cause of the fire remains unclear.

A team of experts consisting of around 100 architects and engineers was immediately convened under the leadership of architect Manfred Wehdorn. By December 22, 1992, a provisional roof and heating system had been installed to keep the waterlogged stucco from freezing. By the spring of 1993, a study of the building's architectural history had been completed. Following a heated discussion of whether to restore or completely rebuild the Redouten-säle, a compromise was reached: the Kleiner Redouten-saal was restored to its original state, while the Grosse Redoutensaal was rebuilt, using modern technology. All the levels were connected with stairways and elevators. The booths for interpreters and audio engineers were hidden behind one-way mirrors.

In order to restore the Grosser Redoutensaal to one of its original uses – as a venue for operatic performances – it was given an orchestra pit that can be covered when not in use. Josef Mikl won an international competition to provide art for the decoration. By finishing the attic, the amount of available space was increased from 7500 to almost 11,200 m^2 (80,000 to 120,000 square feet). The Redoutensäle were formally reopened on October 26, 1997, with a performance by the Vienna State Opera.

saying about the Congress of Vienna having "danced" rather than "met" recalls the numerous (and very lavish) events staged during the Congress (1814–1815).

In 1961 the Redoutensäle were the venue for a summit conference between American President John F. Kennedy and his Soviet counterpart, Nikita S. Khrushchev. In 1973, the halls were remodeled to create a conference center, and in 1979 US President Jimmy Carter and the head of state of the USSR, Leonid Brezhnev, signed the SALT II treaty there. Following a devastating fire in November 1992, the halls were either restored to their original state or renovated.

The Blue Ball is an eyecatcher in the attic, finished after the 1992 fire

The architect Manfred Wehdorn remodeled the attic to create a space of 3500 m² (38,000 square feet). An eye-catcher is the top floor with its Blue Ball. A glassed area of the roof looking towards the courtyard of the Summer Riding School offers a fantastic view of the dome of Michael's Gate and surrounding roof areas.

The stucco ceiling of the Grosser Redoutensaal was replaced with a 404 m² (4300 square feet) abstract oil painting by Josef Mikl in memory of the Austrian journalist, critic, playwright and poet Karl Kraus: the painter used a typical "scrawl," which the viewer can hardly read, to write out the 34 verses of the poem "Jugend" ("Youth"). In Mikl's 22 paintings on the walls, he depicts scenes from works by his favorite authors: Elias Canetti, Johann Nestroy and Ferdinand Raimund.

After the facility reopened in 1998, the Vienna Congress Centre Hofburg Management Company Ltd. assumed managerial responsibility for the Redoutensäle. Nine conference areas offer meeting facilities for up to 1300 participants. The Redoutensaal Wing is directly connected to the ➤ **Hofburg Congress Centre.**

Sammlung alter Musikinstrumente (Collection of Ancient Musical Instruments)

ADDRESS: Neue Burg (Middle Gate), Heldenplatz
OPENING TIMES: daily except Tuesday 10 a.m. to 6 p.m.
PHONE: +43/1/525 24-471
INTERNET: www.khm.at, E-MAIL: info.sam@khm.at

The Collection of Ancient Musical Instruments was founded with two significant 16th-century inventories: the Kunst- und Wunderkammer (arts and natural wonders room) of Archduke Ferdinand at Ambras Castle in Tirol and the art collection of the House of Este at Catajo Castle near Padua. The collection of Renaissance instruments, some of which are true rarities, makes this collection of the ➤ **Kunsthistorisches Museum** one of the most important in the world. In 1947, it was installed on the upper floor of the Neue Burg close to the ➤ **Hofjagd- und Rüstkammer (Collection of Arms and Armour)**. In contrast to earlier systems of displaying instruments (in which instruments were grouped according to the way they produced a tone), the permanent exhibition, which was reorganized in 1993 according to musical periods, takes us through the history of instrument-making and thus of music itself and the most important Austrian composers.

Tour: Our point of departure is the right side-gallery, which explains the origins of music in prehistoric times. To be seen here (and thanks to the audio guide, to be heard as well) are a bone pipe (16,000–10,000 BC), a clay pipe and a fibula (around 600–500 BC). The first three rooms are related to Emperor Maximilian I, who founded the Hofburg Chapel and thus also the institution of the Wiener Sängerknaben (Vienna Boys' Choir), and three other emperors who were composers themselves: Ferdinand III, Leopold I and Joseph I. One of the most precious items is a cittern

Tangent piano by Christoph Friedrich Schmahl (1798)

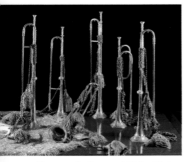

Trumpets by Franz and Michael Lei-
chamschneider (1741 and 1746)

made in Brescia in 1574 by Girolamo de Virchi for Archduke Ferdinand.

A room is dedicated to each of the great composers of the Vienna classic period: Josef Haydn, Wolfgang Amadeus Mozart and Ludwig van Beethoven. Along with fortepianos and various other instruments (including the hurdy-gurdy, tangent piano, baryton, keyed trumpet, glass harmonica, basset horn and clarinet), there are also portraits and busts. The next rooms are dedicated to the Biedermeier period (Franz Schubert), Romantic period and Viennese dance music (Johann Strauss the Elder and the Younger, Joseph Lanner, Johann Schrammel). The 20th century is treated in a rather cursory manner: our journey through time ends with the twelve-tone technique of Arnold Schoenberg and a synthesizer as the supposedly "only new instrument of our time."

Schatzkammer (Treasury)

ADDRESS: Schweizerhof (Swiss Court)
OPENING TIMES: daily except Tuesday 10 a.m. to 6 p.m.
PHONE: +43/1/525 24-486
INTERNET: www.khm.at
E-MAIL: info.kk@khm.at

There's a good reason why the entrance to the Treasury is protected by a massive safe-door in the Schweizerhof (Swiss Court). The objects that are stored there – jewels, medals, vestments, weapons, insignia and liturgical implements – are not only of extremely high material and symbolic value, they also reflect a millennium of European history.

The Secular Treasury holds the most important royal treasures that have been preserved from the Middle Ages: the insignia and jewels of the Holy Roman Empire, including the Imperial Crown. It was made in the second half of the 10th century, presumably for the coronation of Otto I in 962. The octagonal body is formed by eight gold plates set with precious stones and pearls, representing heavenly Jerusalem with its eight gates. The large brow and neck plates have 12 large precious stones each as symbols of the 12 Apostles and the Tribes of Israel. Among the imperial insignia are the golden Imperial Orb (around 1200), the Gothic Scepter, the Aspergilum (container used for sprinkling holy water on the altar), the Imperial Sword (blade from the 4th quarter of the 11th century), the Imperial Cross made around 1024–1025 and the Holy Lance. The leather cases in which the imperial jewels were kept can also be seen (Rooms 11 and 12). The set of coronation robes in the Secular Treasury provides a unique example of medieval textile artistry.

Because the imperial jewels did not belong to the Emperor even after his coronation (they were kept in Nuremberg from 1424 to 1796), the rulers had their own insignia made. Most of them got broken, but the Crown of Rudolf II by Jan Vermeyen of Antwerp (made between 1598 and 1602) survived the centuries. Between 1612 and 1615, Emperor Matthias, Rudolf's brother and successor, had a matching scepter and imperial orb made by Andreas Osenbruck. This set became the official insignia of the monarchy in 1804, when Emperor Francis II proclaimed the Hereditary Empire of Austria (thus becoming Francis I). The Crown, Scepter and Imperial Orb are in Room 2, together with Friedrich von Amerling's 1832 portrait of Francis wearing the Imperial Robes. The mantle with a train (1830) of red velvet has an ermine collar and is embroidered in gold. It can be seen in Room 3.

The Austrian Archducal Crown that was made in 1616 is kept at Klosterneuburg Abbey near Vienna, but the Scepter and the Imperial Orb are in the Treasury (both from the 14th century). They can be seen in Room 9 within the context of the Bohemian Elector's Robes. Another Archducal Crown was made for Joseph II in 1764, but only the carcass has been preserved (Room 1). Rooms 15 and 16 present the Liturgical Vestments and other precious items from the Order of the Golden Fleece as well as numerous memen-

The Crown of the Holy Roman Empire (2nd half of the 10th century)

tos of the Habsburgs and other dynasties.

The Ecclesiastical Treasury holds the liturgical implements of the ➤ **Hofburg Chapel** and religious memorabilia of the Habsburgs. The liturgical vestments, chalices, house altars, crucifixes, monstrances, lamps, reliquaries, Madonna statuettes and so on are in the old Rooms I–V with their tunnel vaulting and paneling. The large display cases are from the Baroque period. One of the most beautiful objects is the 123-cm (48-inch) copy of the Column to the Virgin Mary found on the square Am Hof in Vienna. It was made by Philipp Küsel around

Emperor Charles VI in the regalia of the Order of the Golden Fleece (c. 1730)

1670-80 of gilt silver decorated with painted enamel, precious stones and pearls.

History: As early as the beginning of the 14th century, at least part of the Habsburg's treasures must have been in the Hofburg, more precisely in the sacristy of the Hofburg Chapel. Under Ferdinand I a treasury was built in the northwestern wing with its Schweizertor (Swiss Gate). It was remodeled and completed between 1551 and 1554. Rudolf II,

The Orb of the Holy Roman Empire (around 1200)

whose residence was in Prague, built a wing between 1583 and 1585 that was first called Kunsthaus (Art House) and later Schatzkammer (Treasury) It adjoined the north tower of the fortress on the northeast. Even though the Treasury was moved several more times (e. g. because the three-storey gallery wing needed renovation), it stands in approximately the same place now as then. Access was via the Säulenstiege (Pillar Staircase) and through an iron door bearing the monogram of Charles VI (two intertwined Cs) and the date 1712. The lock is said to have been the most complicated one in Vienna.

Maria Theresa, a daughter of Charles VI, had her treasurer, Joseph Angelo de France, redisplay the holdings of the Secular Treasury between 1747 and 1750 (the rooms that were used for that purpose at the time are now part of the Ecclesiastical Treasury). Under Joseph II, Maria Theresa's son, the two collections were administratively separated after the Emperor transferred responsibility for the Ecclesiastical Treasury to the Hofburg parish priest in 1782. Because it was feared that the Treasure of the Order of the Golden Fleece could fall into the hands of Napoleon, it was moved from Brussels to Vienna in 1794. The Imperial Jewels were also moved from Aachen and Nuremberg in 1796 and placed in the Treasury in 1800 on the orders of Emperor Francis II. There they remained until the Holy Roman Empire was dissolved in 1806. When the imperial collections were reorganized under Francis Joseph in 1891, all the remaining art objects

Copy of the Column to the Virigin Mary by Philipp Küsel (c. 1670)

in the Treasury were transferred to the newly opened ➤ **Kunsthistorisches Museum**. The Treasury had already undergone a reorganization in 1886. The downfall of the monarchy was followed by further losses: Emperor Charles and his family took their private jewelry into exile with them. In addition, the Treaty of Saint-Germain specified that the robes and insignias of Napoleon as king of Italy had to be returned to that country. To Hungary went the robes and the diamond-encrusted cross of the Order of St. Stephen. Following the annexation of Austria in 1938, Adolf Hitler took the insignia and jewels of the Holy Roman Empire to Nuremberg, and the Treasury was closed.

In 1946, the insignia and jewels were returned to Vienna, and in 1952 the holdings of the Secular and Ecclesiastical Treasuries were reunited. Additional rooms in the eastern part of the Schweizerhof (Swiss Court) were adapted for the objects of the Secular Treasury. In 1954, the Treasury reopened. Between 1984 and 1987, there was further renovation (including putting the entrance under the stairway to the Hofburg Chapel).

Schmetterlinghaus/Palmenhaus (Butterfly House/Palm House)

ADDRESS: Burggarten
OPENING TIMES: November to March 10 a.m. to 3:45 p.m. April to October weekdays 10 a.m. to 4:45 p.m., Saturday, Sunday and holidays 10 a.m. to 6:15 p.m.
PHONE: +43/1/533 85 70
INTERNET: www.schmetterlinghaus.at
E-MAIL: schmetterling@netway.at

Between 1902 and 1906, the Palmenhaus (Palm House) in the former Imperial Garden was built by Court Architect Friedrich Ohmann parallel to the Augustinian Bastion, replacing two glasshouses. The terrace and the double stairway date from the year 1909, and the additions on the side from 1910. A one-storey connecting corridor to the Hofburg was torn down in 1918 because it disturbed Archduke Francis Ferdinand's view of the back of the Court Library.

The Neue Wintergarten, as the symmetrical Palmenhaus was first called, was considered an important example of Jugendstil glasshouse architecture. To the left and right of the high central section – a vaulted metal construction with a projecting stone façade (Ionic colonnade between rusticated pillars) – are two glassed wings with a sweeping stone balustrade. Masonry pavilions with rounded arches and stucco female figures are at the two ends.

In the 1980s, the Palmenhaus had to be closed for safety reasons. In 1998, following complete renovation, it reopened. There is a café-restaurant in the central section, a plant-storage facility operated by the Federal Garden Administration and the 280-m² (3000 square-foot) Schmetterlinghaus (Butterfly House). Hundreds of exotic butterflies live here in an almost natural tropical environ- ment with a waterfall and small pools (temperature around 26°C or 79°F, humidity about 80 percent). The insects, all of which are bred here and are not endangered species, originally came from tropical butterfly farms in Thailand, Belize, Costa Rica and the Philippines. One of the most impressive species that can be admired here in its rain-forest setting is the Atlas moth, which has a wingspan of up to 30 centimeters (12 inches).

In the Palm House: tropical vegetation and hundreds of butterflies

The Grand Vermeil Service (1808) made in Paris and Milan

Silver Collection

ADDRESS: Michael's Wing (entrance beneath the dome)
OPENING TIMES: daily 9 a.m. to 5 p.m. (July and August 9 a.m. to 5:30 p.m.)
GUIDED TOURS (in German): daily at 11:15 a.m. and 3:15 p.m.
PHONE: +43/1/533 75 70
E-MAIL: info@hofburg-wien.at, INTERNET: www.hofburg-wien.at

Since 1902 the Imperial Silver Collection has been housed on the ground floor of the Michaelertrakt (Michael's Wing). After the downfall of the monarchy in 1918, some of the holdings of the individual court offices (including the Court Kitchen, the Court Confectionery, the Court Cellars and the Court Linen Room) were sold, and the rest were transferred to the Silver Chamber. The imperial porcelain, linens and table decorations have been on public display since 1923. After complete renovation and the adaptation of adjacent rooms that had once housed the Royal and Imperial Gobelin Manufactory, the Silver Room was reopened in 1995 as the Imperial Silver Collection. The admission ticket is also valid for visiting the
➤ Imperial Apartments and the Sisi Museum.
Among the most magnificent pieces in the former Court Silver and Table Room is the Grand Vermeil Service, a completely gilded silver service. It was originally made for Napoleon in Paris and Milan in 1808. Emperor Francis II/I acquired the service during the Congress of Vienna

and replaced Napoleon's coat of arms with his own initials, FIA (Franciscus Imperator Austriae). It was brought to Vienna in 1816 on the occasion of Francis's marriage to Princess Caroline of Bavaria. The set was continually augmented so that the original service for 40 has been increased to 140 today. It is still displayed in the room that was created for it in 1902. The service has a total weight of 1200 kilograms.

In the spring 1814, when plans were being made to hold a huge peace conference in Vienna, the Hofburg did not have a service of precious metal, the flat silver having been melted down for coinage during the Napoleonic Wars. In order to preserve appearances, a completely gilt service was ordered from the Viennese porcelain manufactory. Not until the 1830s was another silver service acquired. The table silver of the Vienna Court was made by Stephan Mayerhofer. It was continually enlarged up to the outbreak of World War I (1914) and is still used today at state banquets.

Between 1821 and 1824, the Viennese porcelain manufactory created a Romantic-Neo-Gothic dessert service commissioned by Emperor Francis II/I. The Habsburg Service, almost all of which has been preserved, was decorated with portraits of the Habsburgs, fortresses and castles, including the dynasty's ancestral seat. In addition to numerous other porcelain services (made by Sèvres, Herend and Minton), cut crystal from Bohemia, table decorations and centerpieces up to 30 meters (100 feet) in length and Japanese Imari porcelain from the 17th and 18th centuries, the Imperial Silver Collection also has the individual set of cutlery in solid gold used personally by Empress Maria Theresa as well as Elisabeth's silver cutlery with a dolphin motif. It was originally made for Achilleion Palace on Corfu.

Terrine and ladle from a service made by Thun (1851); terrine and butter-dish from the service with green bands by Sèvres (1756/57)

Spanish Riding School

ADDRESS: Michaelerplatz 1
OPENING TIMES: Tuesday to Saturday 9 a.m. to 5:30 p.m.,
Sunday 9 a.m. to 1:30 p.m.
PERFORMANCES: in the spring and autumn,
usually on Sunday at 11 a.m.
PHONE: +43/1/533 90 31
INTERNET: www.srs.at

The Spanish Riding School is the only institute in the
world where the Renaissance tradition of training and riding has been maintained and practiced without interruption down to the present day. Training the white horses
takes four to six years. Once they have learned the "natural gaits" (walk, trot and canter) and have been through
their "campagne year" (second year of elementary but
thorough training), they learn more complicated move-
ments, including the pirouette, the piaffe, the traversale
and the passage. Only a few animals have the necessary
talent for what is called the *Schule über der Erde* ("airs
above the ground"), meaning all the figures in which the
horse actually leaves terra firma. These include the levade,
the courbette and the capriole.

The maintenance of this tradition of *haute école* dressage
is in the hands of the riders. There are no textbooks or
written instructions; it is all handed down orally from
generation to generation. The traditional dress consists of

Training in the Baroque Winter Riding Hall: the quadrille

a black, two-cornered hat with diagonal gold trimming, a tailcoat of brown Trevira worsted, and pleated trousers of white buckskin as well as top boots of black leather and white suede gloves.

History: In 1562, Emperor Maximilian II brought the first Spanish horses to Austria because the breed, which was already famous in Roman times, had shown particular talent. Three years later, there is documentary evidence of a "Ross-Tumblplatz" (open practice run) in front of the Stallburg. The first riding hall was built around 1572. In 1580, Archduke Charles founded the imperial stud at Karst near Lipizza (today Lipica in Slovenia, near Trieste) for which he acquired Neapolitan as well as Spanish stallions.

In 1680, Emperor Leopold I decided to build a riding hall on the Exercise Ground (today Joseph's Square). But just before completion, the building was severely damaged during the Turkish siege of 1683 and was never restored. The Winterreitschule (Winter Riding Hall) as we know it today was built between 1729 and 1735 under Charles VI. It was based on plans by Joseph Emanuel Fischer von Erlach. From that time on, the Spanish Riding School got all of its horses from the stud at Lipica. The name Lipizzaner was not used, however, until the early 19th century: up to that time the horses were known as Spanish "Karster."

In 1743, Empress Maria Theresa used the new 55-meter (180-foot) long Winterreitschule (Winter Riding Hall), a venue otherwise used for ceremonial events (weddings, concerts and balls), for the first "carousel" and others followed, including one staged in 1814 during the Congress of Vienna. The last carousel was held in 1894.

After the fall of the monarchy, responsibility for the Court Riding School was assigned to the Agricultural Ministry. The Kingdom of Italy, to which Lipica now belonged, agreed after long and difficult negotiations to allow 87 stallions to remain in Austria. A new stud was built for the horses at Piber (in western Styria). Since June 1920, the performances have been open to the public.

During the Nazi period, responsibility for the Spanish Riding School was transferred to the German Agricultural Ministry in Berlin. The horses of the stud were moved in 1942 to Hostau in southern Bohemia (today Hostoun in the Czech Republic). In a secret operation, the horses

In the Stallburg since the 16th century: the Lipizzaner stables

were evacuated from the front line in 1945 and brought to safety (in 1963 Disney released a film about the dramatic rescue: *The Miracle of the White Stallions*). At the beginning of 1945, the Lipizzaner horses at the Court Riding School were also evacuated. They returned to the Stallburg in Vienna only after the signing of the Austria State Treaty in 1955. In 2001, the Spanish Riding School was privatized, and a year later a visitors' center was opened. There one can watch morning training (irregular schedule, Tuesday to Saturday from 10 a.m. to noon) and take a guided tour of the stables.

Tanzquartier Wien

ADDRESS: MuseumsQuartier, Museumsplatz 1
OPENING TIMES: visitor information/advance ticket sales daily except Sundays and holidays 10 a.m. to 7 p.m.
LIBRARY: Tuesday noon to 4 p.m., Wednesday to Friday 4 p.m. to 8 p.m.
PHONE: +43/1/581 35 91
INTERNET: www.tqw.at, E-MAIL: tanzquartier@tqw.at

In November 1992, several Viennese choreographers called for the adaptation of an old streetcar shed on Vienna's Vorgartenstrasse to be used as a dance theatre. After long discussions, the project was dropped, in part because of the high cost. This, however, did not alter the fact that a dance theatre was needed. In April 1997, the MuseumsQuartier Planning and Development Company suggested the creation of a dance theatre in the former

Imperial Stables. Eventually the cultural department of the City of Vienna was convinced of the suitability of the MuseumsQuartier location. The Tanzquartier opened in October 2001.

The Tanzquartier occupies the second floor of the old building wing between the Main Courtyard and the Fürstenhof. It includes three dance studios, which apart from providing space for professional training and work-shops are also used for shows and lectures. There is also a theory and information center open to the public, with a library, video collection and magazine collection. Hall G is the venue for the Tanzquartier's major events (➤ **Halls E + G**). The season runs from September to April. Pro-grams change weekly, and local as well as international dance and performance productions are presented.

Temple of Theseus

ADDRESS: Volksgarten
OPENING TIMES: no standard hours
PHONE: +43/1/525 24/407
INTERNET: www.khm.at, E-MAIL: info.pr@khm.at

With its simple, rectangular interior, the late-Classicistic Temple of Theseus by Pietro Nobile is a smaller copy of the eponymous Doric temple in Athens. It was built in the new Volksgarten between 1819 1823 to house the statue of "Theseus and the Centaur" by Antonio Canova, which Emperor Francis II/I had seen in the sculptor's studio in Rome and purchased. The sculpture, which was executed between 1805 and 1819, was actually intended to be a symbol of Napoleon. After his defeat, it was reinterpreted as a symbol of victory over the Revolution. Since 1890, the Theseus statue has been an eyecatcher in the Main Staircase of the ➤ **Kunsthistorisches Museum**. Until 1841 a lapidarium with Roman sculptures and inscriptions from the Antiquities Collection was displayed in the (now closed) catacombs of the Theseus Temple. Later the Tem-ple served for several years as a venue for displaying a selection of the finds made in Ephesus starting in 1895. They are now in the ➤ **Ephesus Museum** in the Neue Burg. Today the Temple, which is administered by the Kunsthistorisches Museum, is used only occasionally for small exhibitions and events.

Volksgarten
(Club Discothèque and Pavilion)

ADDRESS: Burgring 1
OPENING TIMES: Club Discothèque: generally starting at 11 p.m.
PHONE: +43/1/532 42 41
INTERNET: www.volksgarten.at, E-MAIL: info@volksgarten.at

Peter Corti was born around 1781 in Bergamo, Italy. In
the summer he ran a coffee house in the Paradeisgartl
atop the Löwel Bastion, and it became an extremely popular meeting place for Viennese society. Between 1820
and 1822, he added a semicircular foyer to the building.
He also built a similar building only a few hundred meters
away in the new Volksgarten. The second Cortisches Kaffeehaus (Corti's Café), a late-Classicistic building with a
glassed-in Ionic colonnade and a terrace with space for
dancing, was built according to plans by Pietro Nobile
and opened on May 1, 1823. The musicians who played
here during the Biedermeier period included Josef Lanner
and Johann Strauss the Elder. In contrast to his first café,
which was ➤torn down in 1872 to make room for the
Burgtheater (➤ **Environs**), Corti's second café remained in
the Volksgarten and was expanded in 1898.
Although severely damaged in the bombing of World War
II, the building was reconstructed between 1947 and 1950
by Oswald Haerdtl, and a restaurant was added. In 1958
Haerdtl remodeled his establishment in the style of the
day and added a conservatory with a retractable glass
roof. For the most part, the remarkable interior has been
preserved. Legendary for the appearances of artists such
as Ella Fitzgerald and Joe Zawinul, the Volksgarten is

now a discothèque. In summer the garden (with colored lamps on the tables) and the columned hall – now called "Banana" – are used for weekend dances. In 1951 Haerdtl added a "Milchbar" and the terrace and outdoor seating area were expanded in 1953. The glass Pavilion with its projecting penthouse roof is the only café by the architect that still exists in its original condition.

Zoom Kindermuseum

ADDRESS: MuseumsQuartier, Museumsplatz 1
OPENING TIMES: daily. Programs begin at various times; reservations are usually necessary.
PHONE: +43/1/524 79 08
INTERNET: www.kindermuseum.at
E-MAIL: info@kindermuseum.at

In 1992, art historian Claudia Haas suggested creating a children's museum in Vienna on the American model. Some 600 m² (6500 square feet) of space was made available in the Fischer von Erlach Wing of the Museums-Quartier, and a temporary museum opened in November 1994. Due to the museum's success, major expansion became necessary, and the Zoom Children's Museum now occupies premises three times its 1993 size in the Fürstenhof. It opened in the autumn of 2001. Each year, Zoom stages two large exhibitions for children from seven to 12 years, in which a topic from the field of art, science or the culture of everyday life is presented in an interactive and playful manner. For kids under six, there is Zoom Ocean with installations and objects. And children from eight to 14 years also have access to the multi-media laboratory Zoomlab.

The Environs
Within Walking Distance

Sights

AM HOF: In Roman times this square was part of the military camp. Around 1155, Henry II Jasomirgott founded the Babenberg capital near what is today the Church of the Nine Choirs of Angels. Following construction of the Hofburg in the 13th century, the mint was housed in the former Babenberg palace. In 1365, Duke Albert III gave the area to the Carmelite order, which built a church and monastery. Today the square with its column dedicated to the Virgin Mary is remarkable for its Baroque architecture. To the right of the Urbanihaus (No. 12, façade in the style of Johann Lucas von Hildebrandt) is Collalto Palace (No. 13), where in 1762 the six-year-old Wolfgang Amadeus Mozart performed for the first time in Vienna. The church balconies are unusual for Austrian Baroque architecture. This was where Pope Pius VI gave his Easter blessing "Urbi et orbi" in 1782 and where the establishment of the Austrian Empire and the dissolution of the Holy Roman Empire were proclaimed in 1804 and 1806, respectively. Between 1912 and 1914, the former monastery building was replaced by the headquarters of the Österreichische Länderbank (now Bank Austria-Creditanstalt). On the opposite side of the square stand the Märklein'sches Haus (No. 7), built between 1727 and 1730 on a design by Hildebrandt – adaptation for the Fire Department in 1935), the Renaissance Schmales (Narrow) Haus (No. 8), the Unterkammeramtsgebäude (No. 9), heavily damaged during the Second World War, and in the north corner the Bürgerliches Zeughaus, which since 1884 has been the Central Fire Station. It was built in the mid-16th century and remodeled by Anton Ospel between 1731 and 1732. The sculptures on the façade are by Lorenzo Mattielli. The Fire Department Museum in the Märklein'sches Haus is open to visitors (Saturday and Sunday 11 a.m. to 1 p.m).

ATELIERHAUS DER AKADEMIE DER BILDENDEN KÜNSTE (ACADEMY OF FINE ARTS, ATELIERHAUS): Lehárgasse 6-8, telephone: +43/1/588 16-170. The former storage facility for sets and props of the Court Theater was built in 1873 by Gottfried Semper and Carl von Hasenauer. Now called the Semperdepot, it houses several of the Academy's classes. The impressive Prospekthof courtyard with its four-storey gallery of cast-iron columns and the Malersaal ("painter's hall") are open only for specific events or by appointment.

FEDERAL CHANCELLERY: Ballhausplatz 2, telephone: +43/1/53 115-4012. The Baroque building of the former Secret Court and State Chancellery was built by Johann Lucas von Hildebrandt between 1717 and 1721 and was a central venue for the Congress of Vienna in 1814 and 1815. Since 1919 it has been the office of the Austrian Foreign Minister and since 1922 also of the Federal Chancellor. In 1934 Chancellor Engelbert Dollfuss was assassinated by Nazis in the Marmoreck Salon on the second floor. During the Nazi period the building was the seat of the Gauleiter (district leader). The refurbishing of the Chancellery rooms, which had been destroyed in 1944, was undertaken between 1945 and 1950 by Oswald Haerdtl and Robert Obsieger. As a rule they are not open to the public.

BURGTHEATER: Dr.-Karl-Lueger-Ring 2, telephone: +43/1/51444-4140. The former Hoftheater (Court Theatre) was built between 1874 and 1888 by Gottfried Semper and Carl von Hasenauer in the style of the Italian High Renaissance with opulent decorations in the Baroque manner. The ceiling paintings in the stairwells of the two wings are by Gustav Klimt, Ernst Klimt and Franz von Matsch. The auditorium was severely damaged by bombing in 1945 and rebuilt between 1948 and 1955. Known to the Viennese simply as the "Burg," the theater is one of the most important in the German-speaking world. Tours: daily at 3 p.m. (in July and August also at 2 p.m.), on Sundays and holidays at 11 a.m. as well.

DENKMAL GEGEN KRIEG UND FASCHISMUS (MONUMENT AGAINST WAR AND FASCISM): The five-part group of sculp-

Burgtheater: one of the two wings with grand staircases

tures is on Albertinaplatz, where the Philipphof building stood until it was destroyed by incendiary bombs in 1945, killing hundreds of people in the cellars. The sculptures were created between 1983 and 1991 by Alfred Hrdlicka. Behind the "Tor der Gewalt" ("Gateway of Violence") is a bronze sculpture of a Jewish man bound in barbed wire and washing the street. The male figure emerging from a block of marble "Orpheus betritt den Hades" ("Orpheus Enters the Underworld") commemorates those who lost their lives in the resistance against the Nazi regime as well as the victims of wartime bombing. The group concludes with the "Stein der Republik" ("Stone of the Republic"), a granite stele with the declaration of government that re-established the Austrian Republic on April 27, 1945.

KAISERGRUFT (IMPERIAL CRYPT): Tegetthoffstrasse 2 (Neuer Markt), telephone: +43/1/512 68 53-0. Opening times: daily 9:30 a.m. to 4 p.m. The Kaisergruft in the Capuchin monastery is the most important tomb of a European ruling dynasty. It was founded in 1617 by Empress Anna, the wife of Emperor Matthias. Between 1633 and 1989, 145 members of the Habsburg family, including 12 emperors and 17 empresses, were buried there, generally without their entrails (their hearts are in the Herzgruft (Heart Crypt) of the Church of the Augustinians, their entrails in the Herzogsgruft (Ducal Crypt) of St. Stephen's Cathedral). The impressive double sarcophagus for the imperial couple Maria Theresa and Francis Stephen was designed, like many others, by Balthasar Ferdinand Moll. Directly in front of it stands the conspicuously frugal copper coffin of Joseph II.

KOHLMARKT: This expensive shopping street has been called Kohlmarkt ("Coal Market") since 1314 and was the place where wood and coal were sold. At the end of the 19th century – once Michaelertrakt (Michael's Wing) had been completed – a wave of construction activity got underway. A number of remarkable buildings were erected at the beginning of the 20th century in the style of the Viennese Secession (for example, No. 2 and No. 9). In 1964-65 Hans Hollein designed the former candle shop Retti (Nos. 8–10) and Schullin jewelers (No. 7). The Imperial and Royal Confectionary Demel was founded in 1786 on St. Michael's Square. Since 1887 it has been located in the former Blankenstein Palace (No. 14), and it remains Vienna's most elegant café and cake shop. The rooms are magnificently decorated in the style of late historicism.

LOOS-HAUS: Michaelerplatz 3, Opening hours of the bank: Monday to Friday 9 a.m. to 3 p.m., Thursday 9 a.m. to 5:30 p.m. The steel-framed structure was built by Adolf Loos between 1909 and 1911 for the men's tailor Goldman & Salatsch. The functional simplicity of the façade above the marble portal originally caused an uproar because of the glaring contrast with the Hofburg's Neo-Baroque Michaelertrakt, which had been completed in 1893, only a few years earlier. For a long time the office and apartment building was considered the major work by Loos and a monument of Neue Sachlichkeit (New Objectivity). In 1989, it was renovated and refurbished inside and out by Burkhardt Rukschcio for Austria's Raiffeisenbank. The magnificently appointed premises are well worth seeing.

MICHAELERKIRCHE (ST. MICHAEL'S CHURCH): The parish and monastery church (Salvatorian order) with a nave and two aisles on Michaelerplatz (St. Michael's Square) is an important early Gothic basilica with an early Classicist façade dating from 1792. It was built between 1220 and 1250 as the town's second parish church (in addition to St. Stephen's). Since the 14th century it has been one of Vienna's most important burial churches and has more than 100 gravestones and monuments. The main altar was designed by Johann Baptist d'Avrange in 1781–1782; the relief of the falling angel, which transitions into three-dimensional sculpture, is by Karl Georg Merville. In the passageway leading from Michaelerplatz to Habsburgergasse, there is a lovely late-15th century Mount of Olives relief.

MINORITENKIRCHE (CHURCH OF THE FRIARS MINOR):
The church on Minoritenplatz (Minorite Square) was
built in the mid-13th century, originally with two aisles.
Construction of the long chancel was completed in 1295.
It was demolished in 1903, and today its location is
marked by inset stones. In the mid-14th century, the
Gothic church with its projecting portal was remodeled,
giving it a nave and two aisles. The tower between the
two chancel apses was once crowned by a slender pyramidal top. In 1784, Joseph II gave the church to the Italian
congregation of Madonna della Neve. The interior, which
had been refurbished during the Baroque era, was later re-
Gothicized by Johann Ferdinand Hetzendorf von Hohenberg, who also designed the high altar. Since 1957, the
Friars Minor have been back in charge of what has
become the Italian church in Vienna. In the left aisle is an
altar of Carrara marble (1845–1847) with a mosaic copy
by Giacomo Raffaelli (1816) of the "Last Supper" by
Leonardo da Vinci.

PALAIS TRAUTSON (PALACE): Museumstrasse 7, telephone:
+43/1/521 52-0. This High-Baroque garden palace with
its mighty central projection and highly structured façade
was built for Johann Leopold Donat Prince Trautson
between 1710 and 1712 according to plans by Johann
Bernhard Fischer von Erlach. Today it houses the Ministry
of Justice and is not open to the public.

PARLIAMENT: Dr.-Karl-Renner-Ring 1–3, telephone:
+31/1/40 110-2715 and -2577. The Parliament was built
between 1871 and 1883 by the Danish architect Theophil
Hansen in the strict style of Neo-Renaissance historicism
as a representational building for the upper and lower
houses of the Austrian Parliament in the days of the
monarchy. A curved ramp leads around the fountain with
a statue of Pallas Athena (by Carl Kundmann, 1898–1902)
to the dominant central section of the building with its
mighty portico façade. Edmund von Hellmer created the
relief in the triangular pediment between 1879 and 1888.
It depicts the granting of the constitution to the peoples of
Austria's 17 crown lands by Emperor Francis Joseph I.
The building was partially destroyed during the Second
World War (reconstruction work lasted until 1956). It is
easy to lose one's way in the numerous corridors. Tours:
generally on weekdays when neither the upper nor the
lower house is in session.

PETERSKIRCHE (ST. PETER'S CHURCH): According to legend, the church was founded in 792 by Charlemagne. Remodeled several times, it was destroyed by fire in 1661. Rebuilding began in 1701 according to plans by Gabriele Montani, which included the dome. The plans were altered in 1703 by Johann Lucas von Hildebrandt. The church, which faces the Graben, was consecrated in 1733 and is considered one of the most important Baroque ecclesiastical buildings in Vienna. The frescoes in the dome are by Johann Michael Rottmayr, the sculptural decoration by Matthias Steinl.

STAATSOPER (VIENNA STATE OPERA): Opernring 2, telephone: +43/1751 444-2606 and -2421. Construction began in 1861 on plans by August Sicard von Sicardsburg and Eduard van der Nüll, who built the first monumental structure in historicism's "Renaissance arch style" on Vienna's Ring as a *Gesamtkunstwerk* ("total work of art"). Numerous artists, including Moritz von Schwind, were involved in the interior design. Neither of the two architects lived to hear the opening performance of *Don Giovanni* in May 1869: contemporary criticism of the building drove van der Nüll to suicide in 1868, and two months later his colleague died of a heart attack. The State Opera was severely damaged by bombing in 1945. It was rebuilt and partially redecorated between 1946 and 1955. Known to the Viennese as the "House on the Ring," the State Opera is one of the world's most important opera houses. Its orchestra is composed of members of the Vienna Philharmonic. Standing room is spectacularly cheap. The social highlight of carnival season in Vienna is the Opernball (Opera Ball). Tours: in summer several times a day on the hour (meeting place: Herbert von Karajan-Platz, first entrance under the arcade).

Museums and Exhibition Spaces

BA-CA KUNSTFORUM: Freyung 8, telephone: +43/1/53 733-0. Open daily 10 a.m. to 7 p.m., Friday 10 a.m. to 9 p.m. Designed by Gustav Peichl and opened in 1985, the Kunstforum specializes in Expressionist art.

GEMÄLDEGALERIE DER AKADEMIE DER BILDENDEN KÜNSTE (PICTURE GALLERY OF THE ACADEMY OF FINE ARTS): Schillerplatz 3, telephone: +43/1/588 16-228. Open Tuesday to Sunday 10 a.m. to 6 p.m. The building of the Academy, founded in 1692, was constructed between 1872 and 1877 on plans by Theophil Hansen. The Picture Gallery on the second floor has a collection of some 300 masterpieces from the 14th to the 20th century (Rubens, Titian, Cranach, etc.). The highlight is the "Last Judgment Triptych" by Hieronymus Bosch. Cafeteria (closed during school holidays).

JÜDISCHES MUSEUM DER STADT WIEN (JEWISH MUSEUM VIENNA): Dorotheergasse 11, telephone: +43/1/535 04 31. Open Sunday to Friday 10 a.m. to 6 p.m., Thursday 10 a.m. to 8 p.m. (closed for Rosh Hoshanah and Yom Kippur). The Museum, which opened in the former Eskeles Palace in 1993, sees part of its mission as bringing people together for changing exhibitions, symposia, readings and concerts. Most of the holdings are from synagogues, houses of prayer and private homes that were looted and destroyed by the Nazis.

KAISERLICHES HOFMOBILIENDEPOT (IMPERIAL FURNITURE COLLECTION): Andreasgasse 7, telephone: +43/1/524 33 57. Open Tuesday to Sunday 10 a.m. to 6 p.m. Since its founding by Empress Maria Theresa in 1747, the former "junk room of the monarchy" has become one of the world's most important collections of furniture. It features the personal belongings of famous Habsburgs and lots of other furniture from the Baroque era to the Jugendstil period. Special design exhibitions.

PROJECT SPACE OF THE KUNSTHALLE WIEN: Treitlstrasse 2 (Karlsplatz), telephone: +43/1/521 89-33. Open Tuesday to Saturday 4 p.m. to midnight, Sunday and Monday 1 p.m. to 7 p.m. The pavilion designed by Adolf Krischanitz is used for smaller, contemporary art projects.

SECESSION: Friedrichstrasse 12, telephone: +43/1/587 53 07. Open Tuesday to Sunday 10 a.m. to 6 p.m., Thursday 10 a.m. to 8 p.m. The Jugendstil building with its filigree cupola of laurel leaves was built between 1897 and 1898 by Joseph

Maria Olbrich. Above the entrance is the often-quoted inscription: "Der Zeit ihre Kunst – Der Kunst ihre Freiheit" ("To Every Age Its Art, To Every Art Its Freedom). It is the permanent home of Gustav Klimt's "Beethoven Frieze," an interpretation of the composer's *Ninth Symphony*.

Galleries

NEAR THE ALBERTINA:
Galerie bei der Albertina: Lobkowitzplatz 1. Open Monday to Friday 10 a.m. to 6 p.m., Saturday 10 a.m. to 1 p.m.
Galerie Wolfrum: Augustinerstrasse 10. Open Monday to Friday 10 a.m. to 6 p.m., Saturday 10 a.m. to 5 p.m.
Galerie am Opernring: Opernring 17. Open Monday to Friday 1 p.m. to 7 p.m., Saturday 10 a.m. to 5 p.m.
Galerie Karenina: Opernring 21. Open Tuesday to Friday 2 p.m. to 7 p.m., Saturday 11 a.m. to 2 p.m.
Galerie Ulysses: Opernring 21. Open Tuesday to Friday noon to 6 p.m., Saturday 10 a.m. to 1 p.m.

NEAR THE STALLBURG:
Charim Galerie: Dorotheergasse 12/1. Open Tuesday to Friday 11 a.m. to 6 p.m., Saturday 11 a.m. to 2 p.m.
Galerie Hilger: Dorotheergasse 5 and 12. Open Tuesday to Friday 10 a.m. to 6 p.m., Saturday 10 a.m. to 4 p.m.
Galerie Hofstätter: Bräunerstrasse 7. Open Tuesday to Friday 10 a.m. to 6 p.m., Saturday 10 a.m. to 1 p.m.
Suppan: Habsburgergasse 5. Open Monday to Friday 10 a.m. to 6 p.m., Saturday 10 a.m. to 12:30 p.m.

ON ESCHENBACHGASSE AND GUMPENDORFER STRASSE:
Raum aktueller Kunst Martin Janda, *Galerie Krobath Wimmer* and *Galerie Meyer Kainer:* Eschenbachgasse 3–9. Open Tuesday to Friday 1 p.m. to 6 p.m., Saturday 11 a.m. to 3 p.m. *IG Bildende Kunst:* Gumpendorfer Strasse 10–12. Open Tuesday to Friday 10 a.m. to 6 p.m., Saturday 10 a.m. to 3 p.m.
Galerie Knoll: Gumpendorfer Strasse 18. Open Tuesday to Friday 2 p.m. to 6:30 p.m., Saturday 11 a.m. to 2 p.m.

NEAR THE MUSEUMSQUARTIER: *Galerie Mezzanin:* Karl-Schweighofer-Gasse 12. Open Tuesday to Friday noon to 6 p.m., Saturday 11 a.m. to 2 p.m. *Galerie Hubert Winter:* Breite Gasse 17. Open Tuesday to Friday 1 p.m. to 7 p.m., Saturday 11 a.m. to 2 p.m. *Layr: Wuestenhagen:* Bellaria-strasse 6. Open Wednesday noon to 7 p.m., Thursday, Friday noon to 6 p.m., Saturday 11 a.m. to 3 p.m.

Index

Picture Credits

Most of the photographs were kindly made available by the institutions in the Hofburg.
Albertina: 54, 55 (3) – Albertina/Andreas Scheiblecker: 41 – Albertina/Shotview TimTom: 56, 57 – Austria Presse Agentur: 49, 128 – Bohatsch Visual Communication (map)/Fatih Aydogdu (adaptation): 33 – Bundesgärten: 42 (above), 44 – Burgtheater/Reinhard Werner: 147 – Filmmuseum: 66 – Ingrid Haslinger/ Marianne Haller: 138 – Heeresbild- und Filmstelle: 70, 118, 119 – Hofburg Kongresszentrum: 72, 127, 130 – Kunsthistorisches Museum: 2, 46, 47, 63, 75, 76/77, 85, 86, 88, 89, 90, 91, 92, 93, 100 (2), 131, 132, 133, 134, 135, 136 – Leopold Museum Privatstiftung: 99 (2) – Leopold Museum Privatstiftung/Peter Rigaud: 97 – MQ/Martin Gnedt: 31 – MQ/Lisi Gradnitzer: 53, 125 – MQ/Rupert Steiner: 7, 11, 50, 59, 69, 84, 94, 102, 103 – MQ/Gerald Zugmann: 21 – Museum für Völkerkunde: 105, 106 – Naturhistorisches Museum: 9, 107, 108, 110 – Österreichische Nationalbibliothek/Bildarchiv: 13, 15, 18, 19 (above), 22, 24, 25, 26, 27, 29 (2), 65, 67, 68, 117, 121, 122, 124 – Österreichisches Theatermuseum: 114, 115, 116 – Österreich Werbung: 4/5 – Ortner+Ortner/Josef Pausch: 30 (above) – Schloss Schönbrunn Kultur- und Betriebsges.m.b.H.: 78, 79, 80, 81, 82, 139 (2) –Wawel Castle, Kraków: 19 (below) – Spanische Hofreitschule: 140, 142 – Thomas Trenkler: 10, 32, 34, 35, 36, 39, 42 (below), 45, 60, 112, 137, 149, 151 – Volksgarten: 144 – Zoom Kindermuseum/Alexandra Einzinger: 145

Layout Map of the Hofburg: Joseph Koó
Chronological Map of Hofburg Construction: Fatih Aydogdu/ Thomas Trenkler

Many thanks to Christian Benedik, Edith Czap, Daniela Enzi, Barbara Goess, Ruth Gotthardt, Josefa Haselböck, Yvonne Katzenberger, Edyta Kostecka, Irina Kubadinow, Annita Mader, Hans Magenschab, Stefan Musil, Hans Petschar, Franz Pichorner, Monika Scheinost, Gudrun Spiegler, Gerhard Trenkler, Ingrid Viehberger und A+S.

ISBN 3-8000-7043-X
Translation: John Winbigler
Cover design: Franz Hanns
Photo: Österreich Werbung / Popp
Printed in Austria
7 6 5 4 3 2 1

www.ueberreuter.at